BEYOND CHILD'S PLAY
Sustainable Product Design in the Global Doll-Making Industry

Sally Edwards

University of Massachusetts Lowell

Work, Health, and Environment Series
Series Editors: **Charles Levenstein, Robert Forrant, and John Wooding**

Routledge
Taylor & Francis Group

LONDON AND NEW YORK

First published 2010 by Baywood Publishing Company, Inc.

2 Park Square, Milton Park, Abingdon, Oxon OX14 4RN
711 Third Avenue, New York, NY 10017, USA

Routledge is an imprint of the Taylor & Francis Group, an informa business

First issued in paperback 2017

Library of Congress Catalog Number: 2009013282
ISBN 13: 978-0-89503-386-4 (hbk)

Library of Congress Cataloging-in-Publication Data

Edwards, Sally, 1957-
   Beyond child's play : sustainable product design in the global doll-making industry / Sally Edwards.
       p. cm -- (Work, health, and environment series)
   Includes bibliographical references and index.
   ISBN 978-0-89503-386-4 (cloth : alk. paper)
 1. Doll industry--Environmental aspects. 2. Doll industry--Case studies.
I. Title.

HD9993.D652E39 2009
688.7'2210685-dc22

                          2009013282

ISBN 978-0-89503-386-4 (hbk)
ISBN 978-0-415-78430-6 (pbk)

Dedication

To my daughter Hazel, who provided the inspiration for this book and asked vital and thought-provoking questions along the way.

Table of Contents

Acknowledgments

This book, which began as a doctoral dissertation, was completed with the support of many people, including faculty, colleagues, family, friends, and the people of the Q'ewar Project and the Käthe Kruse doll company. I am very grateful to Andrea Christenson, the owner of the Käthe Kruse doll company, and her assistant Laura Holzhey, who provided open access to their factory and workers in Donauwörth, Germany. Heartfelt thanks to Julio Herrera Burgos and Lucy Terrazas, the founders of the Q'ewar Project, who invited me to stay at the Q'ewar House and spent many hours sharing the details of this deeply inspiring social development initiative. Allison Brown (Germany) and Shayla Livingston (Peru) provided insights and assistance far beyond language translation and interpretation. I want to thank my dissertation advisor Ken Geiser for his ongoing support of this project. Ken has a gift of asking the right questions at the right time. Our conversations over the years have encouraged and challenged me intellectually. My dissertation committee members Robert Forrant and Margaret Quinn also provided strong support and guidance. I want to thank my colleagues at the Lowell Center for Sustainable Production, especially Cathy Crumbley, Pia Markkanen, Joel Tickner, and Pam Eliason, for listening to my ideas as this project evolved and providing valuable insights, information, and feedback. Susan Paju and Julie Glendon, reference librarians at the Acton Memorial Library, and Jan Hutchins, manager of the Toxics Use Reduction Institute Library, located countless books and articles. Editor Helen Snively was a great help in guiding this project from dissertation to book form. Thank you to my friends and neighbors who truly understand how "it takes a village to raise a child." Polly Attwood, Wendy Sanford, Vicki Gabriner, Connie Griffin, Karen Economopoulos, Joan Celebi, Mary Ann Ashton, and Kathie Watt provided childcare at crucial times so that I could focus on this work. Thank you to my parents, Charles and Lois Edwards, and to my siblings for their ongoing love and support. And finally, boundless thanks to Sally Thompson, who has done so much so that I could complete this book, and who is a daily source of wisdom, love, and support.

CHAPTER 1

Why Study Dolls?

Dolls are beloved objects. Even with trends toward electronic toys, dolls remain an important part of the traditional toy industry. While often critiqued from a sociological perspective, dolls are generally considered to be benign industrial products and so are not usually appraised for their environmental impacts. In this book I investigate doll making in different parts of the world to explore the environmental and social impacts of production and consumption in the global toy industry and the associated distribution of risks and benefits in this system. I use the concept of sustainable product design to examine issues such as materials and production choices, working conditions, and community impacts.

Consider the quotes below from young women on opposite sides of the world:

> I give American Girl much of the credit for my interest in history, ultimately leading to my career as a high school social studies teacher. . . . American Girl also taught me to be independent and to stand up for what I believe in, rather than trying to fit into the mold society creates for young women. I learned that body image is not as important as inner beauty and doing good for others. After all, "Actions speak louder than words."[1]

> I have always loved history and international events, and cultures, so the American Girl stories fit into my interests. Now I work in a field that requires a deep knowledge and interest in history, current events, and global cultures, languages and politics. The American Girls started me on the path to learning about more of the world around me.[2]

> The working hours are long and the pressure is terrible. During the peak season we usually work until midnight every day. We have no day off. . . .

[1]Nicole, age 23. Retrieved July 15, 2006, from the American Girl Company Web site: http://store.americangirl.com/shop/twenty/nicolestory.php
[2]Rebecca, age 28. She works as a counter terrorism analyst for the U.S. Army Europe. Retrieved July 15, 2006, from the American Girl Company Web site: http://store.americagirl.com/shop/twenty/rebeccastory.php

1

The chemical smell is strong at the workplace and you can see paint dust everywhere. . . . I never stopped having stomach aches and dizziness in the first month. . . . The major problem is fatigue. My shoulders are stiff and aching after days and nights of work. . . .[3]

My two younger brothers are in school and I came to work here to support them. But the wages are so low that I have difficulty even supporting myself. . . . My kids are left with my parents at home. My husband and I come from a poor village where nothing grows on the land. We had to leave. We live separately because we can't afford to rent a flat. . . . This factory plays tricks with our time. If we cannot finish the quota, our working hours are deducted. . . . In toy factories you get a better income only during peak season. When the slack season comes, you can't even survive with what you get, never mind saving anything. . . .[4]

Who are the young women making these comments? Nicole and Rebecca grew up in the United States, loved their American Girl dolls, and now credit them for influencing their career choices and values. The anonymous Chinese toy workers, female and in their early 20s, grew up in rural villages and migrated to cities to work in toy factories to help lift their families out of poverty. Many young women in the United States, like Nicole and Rebecca, reap the benefits of consumption as they play with toys such as the American Girl doll; meanwhile, millions of young women in China bear the hazards of production.

Many products now on the market are described as being environmentally friendly or "green." But a product that is truly sustainable is more than environmentally sound. It is also healthy in production and use, and is made in a way that is socially responsible and economically viable. Determining whether a product is sustainable requires considering the social and economic factors involved in production (such as working conditions, health and safety, wages, child labor, gender equity, and community benefits such as fair trade and a living wage) as well as the product's environmental impacts throughout its life cycle.

When I chose to delve into sustainable product design I recognized that an in-depth study of a product would provide a meaningful way to understand the complex constellation of factors that impact product design and the globalization of production and consumption.[5] As I observed my daughter playing with her American Girl doll, I was inspired to study this object. One day she was perusing the American Girl catalog and said "Look Mom, you can buy a kit to clean

[3] Anonymous Chinese toy worker. Quoted in *Toys of Misery: Made in China* (National Labor Committee, 2002, p. 16).

[4] Anonymous Chinese toy worker. Quoted in *Toys of Misery: Made in China* (National Labor Committee, 2002, p. 16).

[5] This book grew out of research for my doctoral dissertation in Work Environment at the University of Massachusetts at Lowell.

your doll's vinyl face!" Knowing that vinyl (polyvinyl chloride or PVC) presents serious health and environmental hazards throughout its life cycle, I wanted to learn the story behind the design and production of this doll. Was this doll as benign as it appeared? Where were these dolls made? Who made these dolls and therefore bore the risks of production? Who played with these dolls and therefore benefited from their use/consumption?

The American Girl doll was a large part of my daughter's life from age seven to ten. In her community of elementary school peers, American Girl dolls were vital currency; she and her friends spent countless hours in imaginative play with them. During the first year that she had the doll, she related to it as her adopted sister, insisting that the doll have all meals with our family, and be provided with high quality "childcare" during the time she was at school.

American Girl dolls, conceived in 1985 as "anti-Barbie," have bodies that are realistic for a nine-year-old girl and are accompanied by books that teach girls about different historical periods. The books are very accessible to young readers; each has a nine-year-old heroine who shows intelligence, courage, and strength in adversity. For feminist mothers looking for appropriate dolls for their children, these products are much more appealing than typical fashion dolls.

My initial research revealed that the doll was made of vinyl and cloth, designed in the United States, made in China and marketed in the United States and Canada. In 1998, Mattel, the maker of the Barbie doll, purchased the Pleasant Company, creator of the American Girl doll, for $700 million (Rowland & Sloane, 2002).[6] This case study provided a prime example of the dominant model of globalization of toy production and consumption in the U.S. toy industry, with design and consumption occurring in the United States and the bulk of production outsourced to factories in southern China.

Through further research on doll making and perusal of toy catalogs I learned of the Käthe Kruse doll company in Germany. This company, in existence for 100 years, is known for its high quality, beautiful dolls. In a way that parallels the radical contrast between American Girl and Barbie, in 1905 Käthe Kruse's doll design of a natural-looking, childlike, cloth doll provided an extreme contrast to the porcelain fashion dolls that were the "Barbies" of that period. Käthe Kruse doll heads were originally made of molded cloth. After World War II, the company, like others in the toy industry, began experimenting with various plastics to manufacture the doll heads. In the 1990s the company developed a line of cloth dolls using natural materials that are marketed as eco-friendly. This second case offered a window into the European toy industry, provided a contrast to the American Girl doll in materials choices, and also afforded an example of regionalized production, as the doll is made in Germany and Latvia.

---

[6]Barbie, Mattel's most famous product, was created in 1959 and is still a major product for the company, accounting for approximately 20% of sales.

A key market for the cloth dolls made by the Käthe Kruse doll company is the Waldorf School community in Europe and the United States; it values simple toys that are made of natural materials and left slightly unfinished in order to stimulate the imagination of a child (Steiner, 1996). The Waldorf School movement is based on the philosophies of the Austrian philosopher and educator Rudolf Steiner. Steiner designed Waldorf education around the concept that children have three fundamental forces—mental, emotional, and physical—and need to be engaged through "head, heart, and hands" (Petrash, 2002, p. 24). Waldorf education does not focus on academic learning for young children; rather, it emphasizes the importance of playing and developing the imagination (Petrash, 2002). Art is integrated throughout the curriculum and students often engage in hands-on activities. Many children in Waldorf schools make cloth dolls that are similar in design to the Waldorf dolls made by the Käthe Kruse doll company.

When I learned of the Q'ewar Project, a social development initiative in Peru that has undertaken doll making, the final piece of my research fell into place. The dolls made at the Q'ewar Project are also Waldorf-style dolls, and are marketed primarily to the Waldorf school community in the United States and Europe. This third case study provided an opportunity to consider doll making outside the corporate context. At the Q'ewar Project, the making of dolls is a means to create "sustainable livelihoods" and provide services to the local community.[7] The project is not profit driven; instead, its primary goal is sustainable community development. By studying the Q'ewar Project I could ask other questions: If the goal of making a product is improving lives rather than earning profits, how would the work environment be designed? What materials would be used? If the product is seen as an object of art whose spirit can be passed on to the consumer, what might this mean for the quality of work and product design?

Thus, I studied dolls that represent alternatives to mainstream Barbie-type fashion dolls. Over a century ago, American women doll designers gave feminism tangible form when they created dolls that were safe, durable, and realistic, in contrast to the unwieldy porcelain fashion dolls imported from Europe (Formanek-Brunell, 1993). The dolls I researched can be viewed as modern-day "alternative artifacts in the commercial world" (Formanek-Brunell, 1993, p. 63), yet they differ significantly from each other in design, production, and consumption.

As I designed my research study, I considered how I could amplify women's voices that are often not heard (through my choice of interview subjects), and also how I could engage a new audience, that of women and girls, in a vital conversation about sustainable production and consumption. Some women and

---

[7]The term "sustainable livelihoods" refers to "increasing the capacity that people have to use resources to determine the shape of their own lives" (Braidotti, Charkiewicz, Hausler, & Wieringa, 1994, p. 90).

girls may not be intrigued by studies of the environmental impacts of cars, computers, or other technologies but they may relate well to a study of a familiar and seemingly benign object, such as a doll, that is part of their daily lives. Many girls and women enjoy dolls, care about protecting the earth, and are committed to social justice, but until now may not have heard a story that made connections among these three elements and resonated with aspects of life that matter to them. By describing the environmental and social impacts of doll making in different parts of the world, I hoped to explain the complex narrative of global toy production and consumption in a straightforward and meaningful way.

IMBEDDED MEANING IN DOLL DESIGN

Dolls are important representations of our material culture as their design embodies cultural values. Historian Miriam Formanek-Brunell (1993, p. 2) describes how dolls can be used as "texts" to shed light upon the intentions of producers. These doll "texts" also provide information about the intentions of designers.[8] Many elements of sustainable product design, such as working conditions, materials choices, and consumer/worker safety can be examined by focusing in on doll design, manufacturing, and use.

Dolls provide a unique opportunity to analyze product design because they are sculptural representations of the human form. Because of this likeness, humans often form emotional attachments to dolls that are unlike our connections to other consumer objects such as our appliances or computers. We are dependent upon many technologies but we rarely feel "love" for these objects, whereas children's dolls often become a beloved and essential part of a family.

Dolls have a wide appeal and a long history. They have been found as far back as 2000 B.C. in ancient Egyptian graves as "shabti" (servants to accompany the dead into their afterlife) and are ubiquitous today in our consumer culture both as children's playthings and adult collectibles (Hillier, 1968). In addition to being toys, dolls are created as ritual and spiritual objects, museum-quality art, collectibles, and commercial objects such as store mannequins. Every culture creates dolls in some form. For example, Japan has a long history of making dolls for both ritual and decorative use. The "hitogata" dolls were created at a time when it was believed that the sin of a person could be transferred to a doll by close personal contact. The effigy was then thrown into the river, carrying away the owner's sorrow (Hillier, 1968). In Ghana, girls of the Ashanti tribe wear carved flat wooden dolls called A'Kua-ba tucked into the small of their backs.

---

[8]For example, Ruth Handler, the inventor of the Barbie doll, wanted to create a three-dimensional doll onto which girls could project their adult selves. In her memoir she describes how she designed Barbie to be "not too pretty" and "not too glamorous" because she wanted little girls to be able to relate to the doll (Handler, 1994). Her initial concept evolved quickly into Barbie as a symbol of fashion and glamour.

This practice is said to train them to produce beautiful daughters and be good mothers (Hillier, 1968).

Dolls present a rich opportunity to evaluate choices and uses of materials. Dolls are made of a vast array of materials: cloth, clay, corn husks, papier maché, wood, bone, shells, apples, spoons, and more recently rubber, celluloid, vinyl, and other plastics, delineating a history of available consumer and industrial materials. Mass-produced dolls represent a tremendous use of resources. For example, over 1 billion Barbies and her "friends" (Ken, Skipper, etc.) have been created since 1959 (Tosa, 1997). Lined up head to toe, these dolls would circle the earth more than 11 times (Tosa, 1997)! Mattel has used over 100 million yards of fabrics to produce Barbie clothes, making it one of the biggest makers of "women's" clothes in the United States (Tosa, 1997). At the other end of the spectrum, craft-produced dolls provide a means of creating sustainable livelihoods in impoverished communities (Helmore & Singh, 2001). Local materials and designs can be used to celebrate indigenous communities, educate outsiders, and bring needed income into a village or region.

Since World War II most dolls are made of vinyl and other plastics, chosen for their durability and supposed safety in comparison to other materials such as flammable celluloid and brittle rubber. Most consumers view dolls as extremely benign; yet, as is the story for so many products, the behind-the-scenes production of the modern plastic mass-produced doll presents serious hazards for workers along the supply chain and presents hazards in use as well.

Dolls are typically gender stratified. Although both girls and boys play with dolls, many more girl dolls are made than boy dolls. Historically, boys have been directed toward male action figures to "teach" them about bravery and to provide an outlet for aggressive behavior, whereas girls have been encouraged to play with female dolls to learn how to care for babies, practice personal hygiene, and play-act dating. This gender typing provides an additional element that makes dolls a fertile arena for considering sustainable product design.

Although it is easy to trivialize dolls as unimportant objects in child's play, it is important to remember that "play" is the "work" of a child. The imaginative play of childhood forms the foundation for the hopes and dreams of adulthood. The toys that children use in play may have profound influences on their ideals and aspirations as they grow into adults.

A BRIEF HISTORY OF COMMERCIAL DOLL MAKING

The German doll industry began in the late 1500s and dominated the world market until World War I (Krombholz, 2001). Germany had abundant natural resources necessary for toy production: mature, dense forests; plentiful rivers for water-powered factories; and large deposits of kaolin and other minerals such as quartz and feldspar for making porcelain. In addition, it had a large and readily available supply of labor and numerous specialized craft guilds. The town of Sonneburg in the region of Thuringia became the center of doll making, and for over a century this town was responsible for the majority of dolls and toys shipped to the United States for Christmas. Dolls were made of a range of materials including wood, "brotteig" (bread dough), papier maché, wax, and porcelain (originated by the Chinese, a porcelain recipe was perfected in Germany in the 1700s). The use of papier maché (consisting of soaked paper, glue and chalk or flour) to make doll heads in the early 1800s revolutionized this industry as it made inexpensive mass production possible for the first time (Krombholz, 2001).

In Germany, dolls were made in work areas in the back of homes and every member of the family participated. In the early 1900s, child labor laws came into effect allowing children aged eight and up to work in the doll trade. Prior to these regulations, children as young as three helped to trim and sand the papier maché pieces when they were removed from the molds. Homes were kept extremely hot to accelerate the drying of papier maché parts as slow drying caused warping. In 1900, a family of four received 50 cents for 16 hours of work during which it could complete 980 doll bodies (Krombholz, 2001).

The U.S. doll industry developed in the mid-1800s and began to create products distinct from those on the European market. Many of the early doll makers, such as Ludwig Greiner, who received the first American doll patent in 1858, were German immigrants from Thuringia who had some knowledge of German doll-making processes. It was not until the early 1900s that American businesses began to compete with the quality of German imports. At that time, American companies made use of the anti-German sentiments generated during World War I to lobby for protective tariffs to keep out German products and to advertise American-made toys using a patriotic theme. Also, an American firm finally produced a bisque (a non-glossy porcelain) that was of acceptable quality and could be used in mass production. The challenge for American firms during wartime was to locate raw materials, as pulp, paper, glycerine, and percale were scarce.

The majority of home-based doll workers in New York City in the early 1900s were Italian immigrants. Children routinely worked alongside their mothers in making doll parts. These workers could never afford to own one of the beautiful dolls they produced for the middle and wealthy classes (Formanek-Brunell, 1993).

Formanek-Brunell contrasts the differences between male and female doll designers in the United States from 1860 to 1914. Male inventors produced dolls using machines and introduced mechanistic qualities to dolls. Because of traditional gender roles and separation between male and female spheres, few men observed children playing and therefore had no idea about how a doll was used in imaginative play. These designers did not understand that mechanizing dolls made them less available to a child's control and imagination. Such dolls were often unsuitable for play as they were heavy and fragile (like the

European imports) and often dangerous for a child to handle. Also, Frederick Taylor Winslow's theories of "scientific management" were applied in these doll factories: male jobs were associated with strength and female jobs associated with dexterity.[9]

In the late 1800s, middle-class, reform-minded women began to critique the dolls imported from Europe and produced in American factories and began to patent their own creations to address five areas of concern: softness, portability, durability, safety, and realism (Formanek-Brunell, 1993, p. 68). As described by Formanek-Brunell (1993, p. 63), many of these women were "maternalists," progressive reformers whose ideas were shaped by what they saw as women's natural abilities to nurture. This fit with Victorian domesticity but gave women moral authority for reform in the public sphere. These women appropriated dolls as cultural forms to advance their feminist social agenda.

Martha Chase was one of these reform-oriented doll designers. She observed her daughters at play and set out to make a doll that was soft, lightweight, and durable and that looked like a child rather than an adult. The Chase dolls were made of cloth and stockinet (a soft, elastic cotton) and could be washed to kill germs. This concern with cleanliness was a major issue in the early 1900s as public health advocates and domestic scientists began to voice the theory that the environment, rather than personal defects, caused disease and poverty and that improved sanitation practices could cure "the ills of industrialization" (Formanek-Brunell, 1993, p. 83). In fact, the Chase dolls were intended to teach personal hygiene. Also, starting in the late 1800s the American middle class was reacting to a period of overconsumption and materialism and what was seen as "European decadence." These simpler, childlike dolls were a response to these concerns.

Not having access to a factory, in 1891 Chase built a workshop behind her house and concerned herself with making dolls that were appropriate for child's play and also ensuring congenial, safe, and healthy working conditions for her employees; thus she created a "workers' culture" (Formanek-Brunell, 1993). Chase encouraged her workers to feel close to the dolls they produced. This was a far different model from the "scientifically managed" factories run by male industrialists. The modern male-dominated American doll industry eventually marginalized these female doll designers and businesswomen, but the doll designs patented by these women had a lasting effect on doll design well into the 20th century.

---

[9]In 1911, Frederick Winslow Taylor, a mechanical engineer, published *The Principles of Scientific Management,* his theory of managing factories scientifically rather than through "rule of thumb" (Taylor, 1911). His goals were to increase efficiency and productivity, but the implementation of his methods increased monotony for workers and removed control from skilled crafts-people to management.

In the 19th century, chemists developed new materials that were eventually used in doll making, including vulcanized rubber and celluloid. Rubber was licensed for making doll heads in the 1850s. Celluloid, a highly flammable material, was first processed around this time and was used as a substitute for ivory and bone. In the late 1800s, it was used to make doll heads as it was light and easy to mold and decorate. However, it was flammable, faded easily, and would crush if squeezed tightly, making it problematic in this industry (Goodfellow, 1993).

After World War II plastics became more widely available. Doll manufacturers worked with chemical engineers and experimented with using plastic for doll heads and bodies. In 1947 designers at the Alexander doll factory in New York City worked with chemical engineers to develop a hard plastic especially suited for doll production; other companies soon followed (Goddu, 2004). Plastic met many of the criteria described above, as it was durable and seen as a safe material, compared to breakable porcelain, flammable celluloid, and brittle rubber. The early plastics, however, were not very stable and deteriorated quickly. Today, much more durable forms of vinyl and other plastics are the most common materials used for doll making. As I will describe in chapter 2, these materials, once thought to be safe, have introduced a new set of hazards into the toy industry.

CHAPTER 2

The Toy Industry Today

I begin this chapter by considering trends in globalized production and consumption and the toy industry's place in these trends. I then discuss hazards in toy production and use. I provide an overview of toy industry statistics and review the regulatory frameworks in the United States and Europe for ensuring toy safety. Finally, I look at citizen activism and corporate responses to hazards in the toy industry.

PRODUCTION AND CONSUMPTION IN THE CONTEXT OF GLOBALIZATION

The highly competitive toy industry provides a fertile arena to evaluate the globalization of production and consumption and the inequitable distribution of risks and benefits. Because the failure rate for new products is approximately 80% and the life of most toys is less than one year (a toy lasting more than three years is considered a "classic"), toy companies are driven to cut costs wherever possible (Stern & Schoenhaus, 1990). To ensure economic gains for shareholders, toy executives routinely make design and production decisions that are not in the best interests of workers, children's healthy development, or local communities (Miller, 1998).

Economist Jean Pyle and sociologist Kathryn Ward (2003) describe four trends in globalization since the late 1960s. First, the World Bank and International Monetary Fund (IMF) prefer to let the market determine economic outcomes. Second, export-oriented production is increasing in developing countries, instead of import substitution. In addition, multinational corporations are expanding into many countries with vast networks of subcontractors, and structural adjustment policies required by the IMF and World Bank are being imposed as a condition for loans.

These trends have many negative effects, and women in particular may bear the brunt of these impacts. For example, as public funding for social services has decreased, women have taken on a larger share of unpaid labor in the home. Families find it harder to survive as more land is appropriated for industrialization and less is available for agriculture. This often means that female caretakers must walk farther to find firewood and water and to grow food for their families (Desai, 2002). Women are drawn into the labor force as low-wage laborers in the toy industry and other sectors; increasingly they are found in the informal sector as maids or sex workers, where working conditions are extremely oppressive (Pyle & Ward, 2003).

Under the current globalization framework, development is a private undertaking, whereas it was formerly viewed as a public responsibility. Advocates of this framework believe that developing countries must successfully participate in the world economy if they are to meet their economic, social, and political goals. A cornerstone of this approach is liberalization, including the privatization of public functions and the application of market principles to trade, prices, and wages (McMichael, 2002).

Many developing countries, eager to participate in the global economy, offer cheap labor, tax incentives, and lax regulations to encourage multinational corporations to locate factories in "free" enterprise zones or to contract with local vendors. This fits the needs of many industries that use a business model perfected by Nike and other companies in the 1980s. This approach illustrates what Auer, Besse, and Méda (2005) term the "vertical disintegration" of the manufacturing process. Product design and marketing, which create most of the product's value, are conducted in the United States and Europe, while manufacturing, the least valuable aspect of production, is outsourced to factories overseas, sometimes including home-based workshops (Auer et al., 2005).

This strategy, often called "the race to the bottom" by globalization critics, is viewed as efficient from a macroeconomic perspective, but does not account for the massive social and environmental costs to workers and communities. Risks and benefits are unequally distributed as workers and the communities where production occurs bear the bulk of occupational and environmental hazards, and distant consumers have the benefits of consumption and low prices.

The toy industry is no exception to this approach. Since the 1960s, U.S. toy makers have looked overseas for countries where labor costs are low and regulations are lax, beginning with Japan, and moving on to Mexico, Korea, Taiwan, the Philippines, Indonesia, Malaysia, Thailand, and China. These choices, dictated by economics, have also played on gender and racial stereotypes. For example, Ruth Handler (1994, p. 10), who invented the Barbie doll in 1959, once said that "Japanese women with their smaller hands and traditionally more nimble fingers were ideally suited for making these tiny garments."

In the 1990s, toy factory owners based in Hong Kong established more than 3000 facilities in China (Law & Chan, 2003). According to the China Toy Association, there are now more than 8000 toy manufacturers in China.[1] Currently,

---

[1] See http://www.toy-cta.com/

approximately 80% of all toys sold in the United States are made in China (National Labor Committee, 2002). Hong Kong, once a toy manufacturing center, is now a center for toy design, development, and marketing. There is tremendous pressure to move toy design and development work to China but language, education, and cultural barriers remain (Law & Chan, 2003).

Wages paid to Chinese workers amount to less than 1% of the toy's retail price (National Labor Committee, 2002). The National Labor Committee, a human rights advocacy organization based in New York City, has found that Mattel spends 30 times as much on advertising each toy as it pays workers in China to make the toy. These stark facts help explain what makes toys "affordable" in the United States. The major toy retailers are Wal-Mart, Toys"R"Us, Target, and Kmart; together they account for over 50% of toys sold in the United States (National Labor Committee, 2002). As labor costs are a tiny percentage of the retail price, manufacturers, retailers, and shareholders pocket the profits from this industry, leaving behind pollution and workers who may have been exposed to toxins, posing unknown risks to their future health.

This globalization model encourages product designs that are anything but sustainable; the focus is on creating cheap products with short lives. Because regulations are lax, the supply of low-cost labor is abundant, and the environmental and social costs are externalized, decision-makers can choose hazardous materials without considering the long-term consequences to workers, communities, and ecosystems.

While multinational toy companies strive to project a public image of wholesomeness, safety, and health to consumers in the industrialized world, many hazards result from this business model. Advocacy organizations brought the issues of sweatshops and toxic chemicals in toys to public consciousness in the 1990s and have continued their activism to the present. Corporations have developed codes of conduct, both individually and in industry groups, but these codes have had limited success in implementation. Even with government regulations, corporate codes of conduct, and the continued vigilance of activists, glaring hazards remain in the toy industry.

HAZARDS IN TOY PRODUCTION AND USE

I've been working since I was 15 years old. . . . I've worked in the spraying department for three years. I've always suspected the paints are poisonous. I've been sick ever since I started working in spraying. (National Labor Committee, 2002, p. 16)

We have seen people faint at the workplace. That's expected. We are tired, we get low pay, we don't eat well, we can't sleep well. . . . You just don't want to eat, being so tired and [working] under such heat. (National Labor Committee, 2002, p. 16)

The quotes on the previous page by young Chinese workers provide a window into the working conditions in toy factories. Over three million toy workers are employed in these factories, the majority located in Shenzhen, a city in the southern province of Guangdong.[2] Eighty-five percent of these workers are young women between the ages of 18 and 30; women older than 25 are not usually recruited. According to the National Labor Committee (2002) and China Labor Watch (2005), China's labor laws are routinely violated. During peak season, employees work 14- to 18-hour shifts, seven days per week, and are paid wages well below the official minimum wage (National Labor Committee, 2002).

Human rights advocacy organizations such as the Hong Kong Christian Industrial Committee, the Asia Monitor Resource Center, and the National Labor Committee have conducted anonymous interviews with toy workers in Asian factories to collect data on working conditions. These interviews reveal that workers are exposed to toxic solvents and glues in factories without sufficient ventilation and receive little training in handling hazardous materials or using personal protective equipment. Living conditions are unsanitary: 12 to 16 workers share one dorm room and 150 people may share a bathroom. The factories are often noisy and hot (or cold) and fire safety measures are poor (Bjurling, 2004; National Labor Committee, 2002; Wong & Frost, 2000).

In 1993 a fire at the Kader doll factory in Thailand killed 188 workers. A case study of this fire by the International Labor Organization found many similarities to the Triangle Shirtwaist Factory Fire of 1911 in New York City. Because exits at the Thai factory were locked to prevent workers from stealing toys, employees jumped from third- and fourth-floor windows to escape flames, resulting in many injuries and deaths (Grant, 1994).

Also in 1993, a fire at the Zhili toy factory in the town of Kuichong, in Shenzhen Province, China killed 81 workers. At the time of the fire, only one of four exits was operational: to control worker movement, two exit doors were soldered shut and two were kept locked. With flammable materials such as chemical fibers and foam rubber stored within the work area, the fire spread quickly. According to a detailed report, no one in management took charge of the evacuation and chaos ensued. Shenzhen fire safety inspectors had inspected this factory in the first half of 1993 and found many safety problems. Remediation of these problems required capital and if implemented would have impacted the production schedule. Rather than ensuring that these problems were corrected, the town government acted on behalf of the Hong Kong factory owner and requested that this factory (and 49 others) be granted fire safety certificates. Bribes were paid to the fire inspectors to ensure that the permits were issued. Tragically,

---

[2] In 2008, 3631 toy companies went out of business and thousands of toy workers have lost their jobs (Foreman, 2008).

this business transaction proved to be at the expense of worker safety, resulting in the deaths of many workers, mostly young rural women (Fu, 1998).

In addition to hazards in production, toys can present hazards in use, in spite of government regulations enacted to ensure their safety. The leading cause of deaths from toys is choking on small parts, but toys may present other serious hazards such as strangulation and loud noises (Cassady, 2005). Projectile toys and scooters pose additional safety hazards. In addition, toxic chemicals used in the production process may create hazards in use, in particular, heavy metals such as lead and cadmium, and phthalates, a class of chemicals commonly used to soften plastic made of polyvinyl chloride (PVC). Some other chemicals of concern include textile dyes (some azo dyes are carcinogens), pesticides, brominated flame retardants (found in some foam products for infants, such as pillows), and toluene and xylene (found in some children's nail polish). I discuss lead and phthalates in some detail below.

Lead is toxic to the nervous system and also impacts renal function. Children who are chronically exposed to low lead levels experience learning disabilities and behavior changes (Sanborn, Abelsohn, Campbell, & Weir, 2002). Lead may be present in painted toys, in children's jewelry, and as an additive in plastic as a heat stabilizer or coloring agent. In the United States the current federal standard for lead in paint is 600 parts per million.[3] In the summer of 2007, a series of voluntary toy recalls brought attention to lead on the surface paint of toys. First, RC2 Corporation recalled 1.5 million "Thomas and Friends" wooden railway toys that violated the lead paint standard.[4] This was followed by six recalls by Mattel and Fisher Price in August, September, and October 2007 for violations of the lead standard on the surface paint of over two million toys. By the end of 2007, the U.S. Consumer Product Safety Commission (CPSC) announced 42 recalls for violation of the lead paint standard, involving more than twenty toy companies.[5]

Although lead in toys received much media attention in 2007, this is not a new problem. Approximately 60% of the recalls over the last two decades that were related to manufacturing problems involved lead paint (Bapuji & Beamish, 2007). Although on paper China's lead paint standard for consumer products (90 parts per million) is stricter than that of the United States, this law is not strongly enforced. In China, much of the paint used for industrial purposes (such as painting bridges and cars) contains high lead levels. Such paint is up to one-third

---

[3]Federal legislation signed into law in August 2008 lowers the standard for lead in children's products to 300 parts per million in one year, and 100 parts per million in three years. The lead in paint standard has been lowered to 90 parts per million as of August 2009.

[4]This recall occurred on June 13, 2007. An additional 200,000 Thomas and Friends toys were recalled on September 26, 2007.

[5]See http://www.cpsc.gov/cpscpub/prerel/category/toy.html

cheaper than non-leaded paint, produces richer colors, and is easier to apply—and may find its way into toy factories (Barboza, 2007).

Some large multinational toy companies have attempted to put systems in place to ensure quality; for example, Mattel has certified eight paint suppliers. Still, factory operators are under extreme pressure to cut costs and may do so by purchasing cheaper, substandard materials from their subcontractors, such as highly leaded paint. In the summer of 2007, two of Mattel's long-time contractors broke the company rules by using a non-certified paint supplier when supplies ran out (Story, 2007).

Lead is also found in children's jewelry. In 2006, a 4-year-old boy died from swallowing the charm on a bracelet that came with a pair of Reebok shoes. This charm was found to be 99% lead. In 2006 and 2007 there were several other recalls of children's jewelry, including one by the American Girl company and another by Wal-Mart. A recent study speculates that the lead solder used in China to make inexpensive children's jewelry may come from electronic waste (Weidenhamer & Clement, 2007). Many computers are recycled in China and the scrap lead solder reclaimed from circuit boards may be sold to jewelry manufacturers.

The hazards of phthalates became widely recognized in the late 1990s and their use in children's products continues to be controversial. These chemicals, commonly used as plasticizers to soften toys made of polyvinyl chloride (PVC), are not bound in the plastic polymer and so may be ingested if a child mouths the toy. In animal studies, these chemicals have been found to damage the liver, kidney, heart, and lung; they are also reproductive and developmental hazards (DiGangi, Schettler, Cobbing, & Rossi, 2002). In the late 1990s Greenpeace organized a campaign to call attention to the hazards of phthalates in toys. In 1999, acting on the precautionary principle, the European Commission temporarily banned the use of phthalates in children's toys. Three phthalates (DEHP, DBP, and BBP) were banned in all PVC toys and three others (DINP, DIDP, and DNOP) were banned in toys intended to be placed in the mouth of children under 3 years of age.[6] In 2005 the EU ministers voted unanimously to make the ban permanent.

In 1998 the Consumer Product Safety Commission (CPSC) released a report about the risks to children from toys made of PVC containing di-isononyl phthalate (DINP). The agency concluded that few children were at risk because the amount they may ingest would not be harmful. The study authors acknowledged that uncertainties existed and recommended that an exposure study

---

[6]DEHP (Bis (2-ethylhexyl phthalate)), DBP (dibuytl phthalate), and BBP (benzyl butyl phthalate) have been classified as reprotoxic substances, category 2. DINP (di-isononyl phthalate), DIDP (di-isodecyl phthalate) DNOP (di-n-octyl phthalate) have been determined to pose a potential risk if used in toys, but scientific information is conflictual or lacking (EU Directive 2005/84/EC).

be conducted to better determine the amounts of DINP that children may ingest during normal teething behavior. They also noted that there was no laboratory test method to adequately estimate the amount of DINP released that correlates with amounts released when products are actually mouthed by humans (Babich, 1998). As a result of this study, the CPSC did not recommend a ban on phthalates but encouraged the toy industry to remove phthalates from rattles and teething toys pending additional scientific study. Many manufacturers voluntarily eliminated phthalates from their products and retailers removed phthalate-containing teething toys from their stores. However, advocacy groups have tested soft plastic toys labeled as phthalate-free and have found detectable levels of phthalates (Cassady, 2005).

The global toy industry has made great efforts to ensure consumers that vinyl toys are safe and that phthalates do not pose a health or environmental hazard. A brochure by the International Council of Toy Industries (ICTI) states that "the toy industry is concerned that parents and consumers are being unfairly targeted and frightened by extremist environmental groups." ("Vinyl Toys are Safe," 2008, para. 6). The brochure goes on to refute the claims of environmentalists, stating that "vinyl . . . has a safety record of more than 50 years" and "there is no scientific evidence that these chemicals put people of any age at risk" ("Vinyl Toys are Safe," 2008, para. 7).

A different kind of toy hazard is the pressure some children feel to participate in the American consumer culture that results in unhealthy overconsumption. For example, some young girls become intensely focused on acquiring multiple dolls and clothes to achieve status in their social relationships with their peers. This behavior can set the stage for a pattern of overconsumption that carries through to adulthood. Juliet Schor (2005) has documented how excessive involvement in the consumer culture can cause emotional problems in children, including depression, anxiety, low self-esteem, and psychosomatic complaints.

THE U.S. AND EUROPEAN TOY INDUSTRY: OVERVIEW AND REGULATIONS

Global sales for traditional toys (such as dolls, plush toys, games/puzzles, and arts and crafts) are over $54 billion (Vernon, Nwaogu, Salado, Peacock, & Hayward, 2004). The overall world toy market is estimated to be approximately $72 billion (NPD Group, 2008). While the U.S. toy industry is the largest player with sales of over $22 billion, the European Union (EU) has a significant presence in the toy industry with sales of over $12 billion; Germany accounts for over 20% of production; other significant European producers include Spain, Italy, and France (Vernon et al., 2004).

Most traditional toy manufacturers in Germany are small to medium-size enterprises with annual sales of $12 million to $60 million and 50 to 250 employees (Vernon et al., 2004). Some of these companies, such as the Käthe Kruse doll company (see chapter 5), have been in existence for many years and retain their traditional approaches to toy making, while also integrating materials such as plastics, which became widely available for commercial applications after World War II.

Large multinational toy companies are predominant in the U.S. and European toy markets. These companies design and develop their toys at their European or U.S. headquarters; manufacturing takes place in Asia where labor and production costs are lower. Since 1997 the EU's production of toys has dropped slightly, likely because of the significant increase in production of toys in Asia, which are then imported to Europe. Another global trend is the increased demand for electronic toys accompanied by a decreased demand for traditional toys; still, dolls remain a popular toy in the EU, commanding 12.7% of the market share among all traditional toys (Vernon et al., 2004). In the United States, dolls accounted for $2.7 billion in 2005, approximately 13% of the market share for traditional toys (Toy Industry Association, 2005). As dolls are one of the most popular types of traditional toys, they are an integral part of many toy companies' profit strategy.

According to the Toy Industry Association (2005), children spend approximately 9% of their leisure time playing with toys, compared to 16% on TV/movies, 6% on recreational computing, 6% on friends, 6% on video games, 6% on music, 6% on homework, 6% on dinner, 5% on recreational reading, 5% on hygiene, and 29% on all other activities. Fifty percent of traditional toy industry sales are for children aged 5 and under. Once children reach school age, technology "captures" a larger portion of their time. The toy industry has adapted to this reality by incorporating technology into a variety of traditional toys (such as talking dolls and interactive board games on DVDs).

An emphasis on consumption is one of the prime features of American culture. Shopping at malls, "big box" stores, and outlets has become a weekend recreational activity. Still, entry into American parenthood can be a shock as vast new opportunities for consumption appear, including all sorts of baby paraphernalia, clothing, and of course toys. Parents want to know that the toys, food, and other items they purchase for their children are safe and may look for assurance through labeling. However, they rarely have information about a toy's embedded social or environmental history. For example, a label reading "parents' choice award" or "not suitable for a child under 3" tells the consumer nothing about the working conditions under which a toy was made, whether hazardous chemicals were used in making it, whether the finished product contains harmful materials, or whether the wastes generated in production were managed in a way that did not harm the environment.

Regulations address some, but not all, of the hazards described above. The two major U.S. federal laws that address toy safety are the Consumer Product Safety Act and the Federal Hazardous Substances Act. These laws are administered by the U.S. Consumer Product Safety Commission (CPSC), a government agency created in 1972 as part of the Consumer Product Safety Act. This statute gives the CPSC the power to pursue recalls and ban hazardous products, including toys. The mission of the CPSC is to "protect consumers and families from products that pose a fire, electrical, chemical, or mechanical hazard or can injure children."[7] Deaths, injuries, and property damage from defective consumer products cost more than $700 billion annually. The CPSC focuses primarily on preventing certain types of toy hazards: sharp edges and points that can cause lacerations, small parts that can cause choking, loud noises that can damage hearing, cords and strings that can strangle, propelled objects that can injure eyes, electrical toys that can shock or burn, and "the wrong toy for the wrong age"—e.g., balloons intended for play by older children that are swallowed by toddlers (U.S. CPSC, 1995).

The CPSC also administers the Federal Hazardous Substances Act (FHSA). It requires manufacturers to label products to alert consumers if a product is "toxic, corrosive, flammable, or combustible, an irritant, strong sensitizer, or generates pressure through decomposition, heat or other means, if such substance or a mixture of substances may cause substantial personal injury or substantial illness during or as a proximate result of any customary or reasonably foreseeable handling or use, including reasonably foreseeable ingestion by children."[8] According to this definition, for a toxic substance to be considered hazardous, it must be bioavailable (it can be ingested or can enter the body through the skin) and the handling and use of the substance must also pose a significant risk of an adverse health effect (Tickner & Torrie, 2008). The FHSA was amended by the Child Protection Act in 1966 and the Child Protection and Toy Safety Act of 1969. Under these amendments toys that present electrical, mechanical, or thermal dangers can be declared hazardous and toys that are determined to be hazardous to children can be banned.

Certain types of toys are subject to additional U.S. federal regulations. For example, nail polish marketed for children may be subject to the Food, Drug, and Cosmetics Act. In addition, some toys may be subject to the Flammable Fabrics Act. For example, Tris (2, 3-dibromo-1-propyl) phosphate was once used as a flame retardant for children's clothing and doll clothing but was banned in 1977 when studies found it to be a probable human carcinogen.

The CPSC is responsible for assuring the safety of over 15,000 products each year, but it is underfunded and understaffed. In 2007, it had approximately 420 employees, far below the 1000 it had when it was formed in 1973. It also lacks enforcement authority. Because it lacks authority and resources, the agency works with industry to develop voluntary standards and relies on companies to test their products and implement voluntary recalls when safety issues are identified (U.S. CPSC, 2003).

[7] http://www.cpsc.gov/about.html
[8] http:/www.cpsc.gov/businfo/fhsa.html

The Toy Industry Association created a voluntary toy safety standard in 1971. In 1976, the standard was published by the National Bureau of Standards of the U.S. Department of Commerce. The American Academy of Pediatrics, Consumers Union, the National Safety Council, and several national retail organizations and toy industry safety experts were involved in developing this standard, which was later published as ASTM Standard F96303. The American Society for Testing and Materials (ASTM) is a national organization that develops technical standards for materials and products. ASTM standards facilitate participation in a global marketplace as ASTM compliance is recognized internationally. The standard includes specifications for toy safety and takes into account U.S. regulatory requirements for toys.

In 2007, there were 81 recalls of toys for a variety of issues: violations of the lead standard, magnets coming loose (causing intestinal hazards), choking, laceration, and other hazards.[9] This spate of recalls heightened a growing recognition that the current regulatory system is not working to protect consumers. Recognizing these problems, in the fall of 2007 members of the U.S. Congress introduced legislation called the Consumer Product Safety Modernization Act to increase the CPSC's budget and regulatory authority.[10] In an unusual move for a business sector, the toy industry asked the federal government to require pre-market safety testing of toys and is working with the American National Standards Institute to develop procedures for toy safety testing and inspection (Lipton & Story, 2007).[11]

Because the federal government has been slow to act, state and even local governments have stepped in to protect children from toxic hazards in toys and other products. In 2006, the city of San Francisco passed a law that banned phthalates in children's products. In October 2007, the state of California passed a law to ban the use of six phthalates in toys designed for children under age three. During the 2007/2008 legislative period, 29 states introduced bills to address toxic chemicals in children's products (Ekstrom, 2008). The state of Washington passed the Children's Safe Products Act in April 2008, which bans phthalates and also limits lead and cadmium in children's products. In March 2008, California Senator Dianne Feinstein introduced an amendment to the federal Consumer Product Safety Improvement Act to ban phthalates in toys and children's products. This amendment remained in the final version of the

---

[9] See http://www.cpsc.gov/cpscpub/prerel/category/toy.html

[10] The House of Representatives passed their version of the bill in December 2007; the Senate passed a stronger version in March 2008. Congress reconciled the bills and the legislation was signed into law in August 2008.

[11] The Consumer Product Safety Improvement Act of 2008 requires manufacturers to conduct independent third-party testing of imported toys to ensure they meet safety standards prior to putting them on the market. The voluntary ASTM toy safety standard is now mandatory.

legislation that was signed in law in August 2008. This new federal law preempts state regulations, though states with stricter standards may apply for a waiver.

Toys produced or sold in the European Union are subject to the Toy Safety Directive (88/378/EEC), which describes health and safety requirements for toys. Toys are defined as "any product or material clearly intended for use in play by children of less than 14 years of age" (Delaney & van de Zande, 2001). The Directive provides guidance in multiple areas: physical, mechanical, chemical, and electrical properties, flammability, hygiene, radioactivity, warnings, and indications of precautions. The harmonized standard for toy safety (known as EN 71) includes eleven parts: physical and mechanical properties, flammability, migration of certain elements, experimental sets for chemistry and related activities, chemical toy (sets) other than experimental sets, the graphic symbol for age-warning labeling, guidelines on finger paints and requirements for testing methods, guidelines on swings, slides, and similar toys for indoor and outdoor family use, requirements and sample preparations, extraction and methods of analysis for organic chemical compounds. The first eight elements have been approved by the EU. The standards relating to organic chemical compounds have been drafted and are widely used, but have not been officially approved (Europe Economics, 2007).

Manufacturers who use EN 71 in the design and production of their toys are presumed to be in compliance with the Toy Safety Directive (Delaney & van de Zande, 2001). To demonstrate compliance with the directive, manufacturers must label their toys with a notation called a "CE mark." This is the manufacturer's self-declaration of safety. In addition, many German toy manufacturers have their products tested for safety by an independent auditor to receive an additional certification known as the TÜV Rheinland GS Mark (TÜV is a globally recognized, independent third-party testing and certification organization). This label verifies that the product was safety tested by an independent third party before it went to market. Most toys marketed in the United States also meet ASTM standards.

In January 2008, modifications to the European Toy Safety Directive were proposed to improve toy safety.[12] This new proposal acknowledges that toys must comply with the EU's chemicals policy legislation known as REACH. It bans carcinogens, mutagens, and reproductive toxins (CMRs) in parts of toys that are accessible to children. European advocacy groups have commented that the new legislation does not go far enough as it does not include a ban on neurotoxins or endocrine disruptors and allows toxic substances in toy parts that are not accessible to children.

Industry representatives agree that aspects of the Toy Safety Directive addressing chemicals should be improved to insure children's health but they disagree with consumer advocates about how to achieve this end. An earlier version of this proposal required manufacturers to conduct a hazard analysis of

---

[12] The European Parliament adopted the revised Toy Safety Directive in December 2008.

each new toy before it is put on the market, and noted that "manufacturers are expected to ensure that toys are designed and constructed so that there are no risks of adverse effects on human health due to exposure to chemical substances or preparations" (Vernon et al., 2004, p. 66). The toy industry commented that risk assessment is more appropriate than hazard analysis and noted that "it is more appropriate to require that relevant substances should not be released in amounts that could be harmful to health than to prohibit their presence" (Vernon et al., 2004, p. 68). Industry representatives also commented that a ban on Category 1 and 2 CMRs would result in most plastics being banned and therefore potentially 80% of toys would disappear from the market (Vernon et al., 2004).

European toy manufacturers may purchase "eco-labeled" fabrics to produce cloth toys such as dolls and doll clothing. In the late 1980s the Austrian Textile Research Institute developed a method to test finished textiles for harmful substances. It joined with German and other textile research institutes to create the International Association for Research and Testing in the Field of Textile Ecology and in 1992 developed the Öko-Tex Standard 100 mark which indicates "Confidence in Textiles—Tested for Harmful Substances."[13] The Öko-Tex 100 standard is designed to protect the consumer of the textile. Finished fabrics with this label must not contain toxic residues, such as carcinogenic dyes, pesticides, formaldehyde, or heavy metals. This is not a quality label, nor does it provide information on other aspects of the product such as fitness for use, reaction to cleaning processes, or flammability. A product with this mark fulfils the conditions specified in the standard under the supervision of an organization that belongs to the International Association for Research and Testing in the Field of Textile Ecology.

Since the Öko-Tex Standard 100 was developed, approximately 60,000 certificates have been issued to 7500 companies in 80 countries, mostly in Europe and Asia.[14] There is growing interest in Öko-Tex certification in the United States. Because of this interest, the Öko-Tex Association held its annual meeting in New York City in 2007.

However, the Öko-Tex Standard 100 focuses only on the finished product, not on the production process. Recognizing this limitation, in 1995 the organization developed the Öko-Tex Standard 1000, which emphasizes environmentally sound textile production processes. This certification requires an independent audit of facilities to assure that harmful chemicals and production processes are eliminated. Facilities with this certification may use a label that specifies that they are an "eco-friendly factory." As of October 2007, 35 Öko-Tex Standard 1000 certificates had been issued to European manufacturers.[15]

---

[13] See http://www.oeko-tex.com/en/main.html
[14] See http://www.oeko-tex.com/OekoTex100_PUBLIC/index.asp
[15] See http://www.oeko-tex.com/xdesk/ximages/470/17254_cilander10.pdf

ACTIVISM TO IMPROVE TOY SAFETY

Advocacy organizations in Europe, the United States, and Asia are campaigning actively to improve toy safety. In Asia, since the early 1990s, the focus has been on securing better working conditions in toy factories. In Europe, campaigns have focused on exposing sweatshops as well as improving consumer safety, whereas the U.S. toy campaigns have focused primarily on child safety.

The catastrophic toy factory fires that occurred in Thailand and China in 1993 catalyzed an international movement to improve working conditions in the toy industry (Bjurling, 2004). In Hong Kong, the Hong Kong Christian Industrial Committee (HKCIC) and Asia Monitor Resource Center (AMRC) have led the effort to investigate conditions in Chinese toy factories. SwedWatch and the Fair Trade Center based in Sweden have worked with the HKCIC to document conditions. In addition, the International Labor Committee and China Watch, both based in New York City, have conducted investigations.

The results of these investigations formed the basis for toy campaigns that have been conducted in Ireland, Germany, France, Sweden, and Belgium since the mid-1990s (Bjurling, 2004). The Irish Toy Campaign of 2003 entitled "Fair Play for Toy Workers" was initiated by the Irish Congress of Trade Unions and Trócaire, an international development organization run by the Catholic Church in Ireland.

The German Fair Toys Campaign, Aktion "Fair Spielt" (Action Fair Play) is being implemented by several non-governmental organizations (the Nuremberg Fair Toys Alliance and Werkstatt Ökonomie, which also coordinates the campaign) and Catholic organizations (the German Catholic Bishops' Organization for Development Cooperation, the Catholic Workers' Movement of Germany, and the Catholic Women's Association of Germany).[16] The "patron" of the German Fair Toys Campaign is Christa Nickels, a member of the German Parliament, and chair of its Committee on Human Rights and Humanitarian Aid. In addition, Renate Künast, Federal Minister for Consumer Protection, launched a "Simply Fair Buy Smart" campaign in 2004. This campaign calls for toy labeling that clearly demonstrates that companies are in compliance with the International Council of Toy Industries (ICTI) Code of Business Practices described later in this chapter. The German Fair Toys campaign has urged toy manufacturers and importers to ensure safe working conditions throughout their supply chains. As of 2004, eighteen German toy manufacturers had agreed to audit their suppliers in China and adhere to the ICTI Code of Business Practices.

As a result of this activism, over the past decade some improvements have been made in fire safety and provision of protective clothing in Chinese factories, but many hazards remain (Bjurling, 2004). A key demand of many advocacy groups campaigning for improved working conditions in the toy sector is to involve workers in implementing and monitoring codes of conduct (Bjurling,

[16] See Aktion Fair Spielt: http://www.woek.de/

2004; Wong & Frost, 2000). Recent audits have determined that many workers are not informed about codes of conduct or standards and are therefore unable to be involved in implementation or monitoring (International Center for Corporate Accountability [ICCA], 2008).

Greenpeace initiated the Play Safe campaign in the late 1990s to call attention to the hazards of polyvinyl chloride (PVC) and phthalates in soft plastic baby toys. As noted earlier, this campaign helped bring about a ban on the use of phthalates in the EU. Another advocacy group, the U.S. Public Interest Research Group (PIRG), publishes an annual report on toy safety to call consumers' attention to toy hazards. Recently, activists in the United States have renewed pressure on manufacturers and vendors to remove PVC and phthalates from children's toys and other consumer products. For example, in 2005 the Center for Health, Environment, and Justice began a campaign called "PVC the poison plastic" to educate consumers and pressure manufacturers and retailers to make changes. As of early 2008, major retailers including Wal-Mart, Target, Sears Holding (including Kmart), and Toys"R"Us have responded to this pressure by announcing plans to phase out PVC in many of their consumer products, including toys and children's products (Pereira, 2008; Toys"R"Us, 2008).

Although the term "fair trade" is usually applied to commodities such as coffee, bananas, and cocoa and is oriented toward ensuring a fair price for disadvantaged growers in developing countries, this concept can also be applied to toys and other types of consumer products produced in developing countries. The Fair Trade Federation (FTF), an organization that includes wholesalers, retailers, and producers, is committed to supporting fair wages and employment opportunities for farmers and artisans worldwide who are economically disadvantaged.[17] This organization has developed principles to identify fair trade organizations and products.

IFAT, an international network of fair trade organizations, also has developed principles for fair trade. IFAT describes a key principle of fair trade as "payment of a fair price." This means that the price of the product "covers not only the cost of production but enables production which is socially just and environmentally sound."[18] In chapter 3, I outline a framework for sustainable product design that encompasses some of the key concepts and principles that have been delineated for fair trade.

CORPORATE RESPONSES

The major corporate response to addressing the problem of substandard working conditions in toy factories has been to develop and implement voluntary codes of conduct through the International Council of Toy Industries (ICTI),

[17] See http://www.fairtradefederation.org/
[18] See http://www.ifat.org/

an international association of toy trade organizations. According to its Web site "the health and safety of children throughout the world is the driving force behind ICTI, which promotes international toy safety standards and a responsible attitude to advertising and marketing to children."[19] In 1995, under pressure from advocacy organizations and trade unions, ICTI adopted a code of conduct. The ICTI Code of Business Practices addresses labor issues (e.g., no underage workers, no forced or prison labor, payment of legally mandated wages and overtime) and workplace safety (e.g., lighting, ventilation, medical assistance, emergency exits, personal protective equipment, clean and safe dormitories). ICTI encourages member companies to adhere to this code of conduct.

ICTI has also developed a monitoring process called CARE that allows a factory to be certified as being in compliance with its Code of Business Practices. ICTI has identified accredited audit firms to be used in the certification process and maintains a list of certified factories on its Web site. A question on its Web site asks: "Isn't having ICTI oversee the process a bit like having the fox guard the henhouse?" ICTI replies that "the toy industry has a long and successful history of taking effective action on important public policy issues, including product safety, product marketing, and worker safety. By promulgating the ICTI Code and supporting development of the CARE process, the toy industry has reinforced its commitment to operate in a socially responsible manner" (International Council of Toy Industries [ICTI], 2008, para. 8). However, in reality, the ICTI Code has been far from successful in improving working conditions in toy factories.

It is widely recognized that audits have limited effectiveness in ensuring compliance with standards. Consulting practices do a brisk business helping factory managers to "pass" the audits (Roberts & Engardio, 2006). Factories are generally given 10 to 20 days' notice before a visit (National Labor Committee, 2002). During this period, the factory and dormitories are spruced up, the assembly line is slowed down, and overtime is cut back. Workers may be given a "cheat sheet" so they can memorize answers to questions about wages and working conditions, and if they answer questions according to this sheet, they receive a bonus (National Labor Committee, 2004). The National Labor Committee (2002) has documented that many factories keep two sets of books with fake payroll lists to show to auditors.

In a well researched book, Dr. S. Prakash Sethi (2003), a professor at Baruch College in New York City and an expert on codes of conduct, takes multinational corporations to task for their behavior in the current era of globalization. Sethi describes how corporations ensure that quality standards are met for consumers in industrialized countries, but at the same time are negligent about ensuring the health and welfare of workers making the products. He notes the irony that

[19] See http://www.toy-icti.org/

corporations depend on a democratic system of governance and an open society to thrive in their home countries, yet make tremendous economic profits by shifting production to authoritarian and non-democratic countries that offer cheap labor and lax enforcement of human rights and environmental protection.

Sethi notes how globalization advocates point to the important role of multinational corporations in creating jobs that provide a means for people to lift themselves and their families out of poverty. But at what cost to the worker? Sethi is skeptical of those who "justify inhaling toxic and potentially carcinogenic fumes, eating insufficient and unhealthy food, and living in highly unsanitary and overcrowded conditions as the necessary price of development" (Sethi, 2003, p. 57). He argues that multinationals can improve conditions in factories overseas by providing fair wages and decent working conditions, at very little cost to their bottom line.

Sethi suggests that companies implement voluntary codes of conduct as a flexible strategy to address societal concerns; he sees this approach as more efficient and less expensive than government regulation. However, he criticizes most current codes as being full of lofty intent but short on content, not taken seriously by the company or management, and lacking effective monitoring and verification. Sethi is critical of the toy industry-wide ICTI CARE process as it lacks a third-party monitoring program and is not transparent (Dee, 2007).

Sethi (2003) lists several imperatives for an effective code of conduct: strong performance measures, transparency, independent external monitoring, and public reporting. In addition, any such code must be economically viable for the corporation and provide for workers to receive a fair share of gains from improved productivity if they are responsible for major contributions to productivity and profitability. It must also address issues that are important to workers and engage important constituencies when creating the code and implementation process. Finally, it must be specific so that standards can be measured.

Sethi (2003) advises corporations to develop codes that address relevant concerns of workers and affected communities but to exclude issues that are outside the reach of the company and to define "zero tolerance" issues and consequences for suppliers who do not meet the code. Codes must be translated into a standardized audit tool that allows for objective and consistent measurement. Significantly, Sethi argues that code compliance must be linked to the performance evaluations and compensation of company management.

Mattel is the only multinational toy company that has adopted a code of conduct that includes the elements Sethi believes make a code viable. He was intimately involved in the development of Mattel's code, called the Global Manufacturing Principles (GMP), and oversees its third-party monitoring process. Sethi is the president of an independent non-profit organization, the International Center for Corporate Accountability (ICCA), based at the Zicklin School of Business, Baruch College, City University of New York. This organization is funded by Mattel and was set up to conduct compliance verification audits for

Mattel's own factories and its vendor factories around the world. According to its Web site, ICCA has "adopted strict conflict-of-interest standards to ensure that audits and research are not supported by the corporate interests that we examine."[20]

Since 2001, the ICCA has conducted numerous audits of Mattel-owned factories and its vendors' facilities in China, Malaysia, Thailand, and Mexico. According to Dr. Sethi, Mattel factory managers are accountable for meeting these standards, as compliance with the GMP represents 20% of their performance evaluation (along with price, delivery, quality, and development of personnel).[21] Perhaps most importantly, the audit reports are posted publicly on the web. Said Sethi, "nothing is more important than transparency. If you have clear standards and if you have transparency you don't need policing. And that is what you will find in most companies; of course the standards are not clear. Policing is non-existent. So they can claim almost anything they want to claim."[22]

Because these audit reports are publicly available, I was able to review them in-depth to better understand conditions in Chinese toy factories and to analyze whether significant changes occurred over a five-year period from 2001–2006. I discuss these audits in chapter 4.

I now turn to a discussion of sustainable product design. I consider the product life cycle, review the terminology and key elements of eco and sustainable product design, and offer a conceptual framework for evaluating products.

[20] See http://www.icca-corporateaccountability.org/index.php
[21] Personal communication, April 2006.
[22] Personal communication, April 2006.

CHAPTER 3

A Conceptual Framework for Sustainable Product Design

Worldwide, our current systems of industrial production and consumption are not sustainable. As the world's population grows and more countries adopt a Western model of economic growth, natural resources are being depleted rapidly. We read daily in the news of many ecosystems showing stress: shrinking world fisheries, global water shortages, ocean contamination, and global warming. The concept of an ecological footprint is used to measure human demand on the biosphere. It calculates how much productive land and sea area are needed to provide resources and absorb waste. In 2003, the total supply of productive land available was 1.8 hectares per person, but our global footprint was 2.2 hectares per person, indicating that humans are overshooting the biocapacity of the earth. In 2003, the footprint of the average North American was 9.4 hectares per person compared to 4.8 hectares for the average EU resident. Meanwhile, the average footprint of lower-income countries remains approximately 0.8 hectares per person, as it has been for the last 40 years (Living Planet Report, 2006). According to this report, as of 2003, the human footprint was exceeding the earth's biocapacity by 25%. Unless significant changes are made, by 2050 this footprint may exceed earth's biocapacity by 50%. How is this problem being addressed?

Over the last several decades, government and business have touted eco-efficiency as a prime strategy for sustainable production. The World Business Council on Sustainable Development defines eco-efficiency as "the delivery of competitively priced goods and services that satisfy human needs and bring quality of life, while progressively reducing ecological impacts and resource intensity throughout the life cycle, to a level at least in line with the Earth's estimated carrying capacity" (Holliday & Pepper, 2002, p. 15). Eco-efficiency has been translated into a variety of cleaner production strategies within the manufacturing sector, including input substitution, in-process recycling, changes in production processes, improved operations and maintenance, and product reformulation. These approaches have resulted in impressive cost savings and pollution prevention.

However, the strategy of eco-efficiency has proved to be an insufficient response to current systems of unsustainable production and consumption. One problem is the "rebound" effect of efficiency improvements, where the change is undermined by a corresponding increase in consumption (Manno, 2002).[1] Moreover, the eco-efficiency model fails to fundamentally challenge the paradigm of economic growth and increased consumption as the road to prosperity. The United Nations Commission for Sustainable Development has defined sustainable consumption as "the use of services and related products which responds to basic needs and brings a better quality of life, while minimizing the use of natural resources and toxic materials, as well as the emissions of waste and pollutants over the life-cycle of the service or product, so as not to jeopardize the needs of future generations" (United Nations Environmental Program, 2001, p. 12). A sustainable consumption model must address the social injustice that underlies our production and consumption systems and consider how to reduce the disparity in distribution of risks and benefits in our globalized economy.

An eco-efficiency framework does not resolve fundamental issues of design, as it focuses on making existing systems work better—using resources and materials more efficiently—rather than rethinking the whole system. Two leading eco designers, American architect William McDonough and German toxicologist Michael Braungart (2002, p. 76), call for a new approach that they term eco-effectiveness: "working on the right things—on the right products and services and systems—instead of making the wrong things less bad." They note that even the most rigorous eco-efficient business paradigm does not challenge basic practices and methods: a shoe, building, factory, car, or shampoo can remain fundamentally ill-designed even as the materials and processes involved in its manufacture become more "efficient."

Design decisions are made throughout the supply chain for a product, including factors such as materials selection and sourcing and how the product is manufactured, packaged, and distributed. Therefore, design decision makers include a range of actors such as company executives and managers, industrial designers, engineers, purchasing agents, marketing staff, and government policy makers— anyone who makes decisions that influence the allocation of resources (Pearson, 2006). Institutional and individual consumers, whose preferences inform the marketplace, also play a role in design decision making. Rather than designing only for eco-efficiency, decision makers must aim to create products that are truly

---

[1] An often cited example is that of increasing automobile fuel efficiency. Though fuel efficiency increased by 34% between 1970 and 1990, total fuel consumption during the same period increased by 7% because of increases in multi-car families and in vehicle miles traveled (Manno, 2002).

sustainable, which means working to minimize both environmental and social impacts of products (and maximize benefits), while maintaining economic viability. This concept can be better visualized through an analysis of the product life cycle (see Figure 1).

THE PRODUCT LIFE CYCLE

The life cycle for most products is linear, beginning with the design process and including the stages of raw materials extraction, manufacturing, packaging/ distribution, consumption/use, and ending with disposal in a landfill or incinerator. As illustrated in Figure 1, resources and waste are ideally managed in closed-loop cycles, with products being reused, recycled, and remanufactured. Figure 1 also shows materials, energy, and labor inputs, and waste outputs. This "waste" can be in the form of energy or materials, but may also appear as occupational injuries or negative social and economic impacts on the local community, which are difficult to quantify. The environmental and social impacts of a product throughout its life cycle are made up of these various forms of waste.

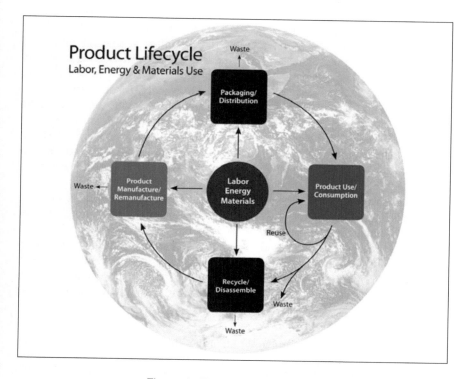

Figure 1. The product life cycle.

Decisions made at the design stage and throughout the product development and production process have ramifications for a product's life-cycle impacts. Extracting and processing raw materials may be hazardous to workers, degrade the environment, and impact local communities. The manufacturing stage poses additional occupational hazards and creates hazardous and solid waste, and air, water, and soil pollution. Packaging/distribution and consumption/use of products often require significant amounts of energy and materials. At the end of a product's useful life, its disposal or incineration may result in health and environmental impacts.

Because products have such wide-ranging impacts throughout their life cycles, it is critical that the design process aim to minimize these effects. Manufacturers are becoming increasingly responsible for the life-cycle impacts of the products they produce, both because of legislation that entails extended producer responsibility (such as the Waste Electrical and Electronic Equipment (WEEE) Directive in Europe that requires electronic equipment manufacturers to take back their products)[2] and adverse publicity that is generated from news about sweatshop conditions or illegal dumping of waste. An analysis of the product life cycle can help make the potential environmental and social impacts visible upfront so that they can be "designed out" to avoid these hazards.

In addition, focusing on design and product development allows us to ask a different set of questions about materials and resource use, production, and consumption. As Hans van Weenen (1997, p. 1) of the United Nations Environmental Program (UNEP) notes, "sustainable product development is concerned with changing patterns of production and consumption. It is resource, context and future oriented product development aimed at providing elementary needs, a better quality of life, equity and environmental harmony . . . this goes beyond eco design which usually focuses on the environmental optimization of existing products." Sustainable design approaches can help spur innovation. Rather than focusing resources on life-cycle assessment, which quantifies and compares the life-cycle impacts of existing products, sustainable product design uses a new set of criteria for creating new products and product-service systems.

Product-service systems are a way of interacting with customers that can enhance the life of the product, increase durability, and ultimately reduce resource use. The United Nations Environmental Program (UNEP, 2002, p. 4) defines product-service systems as "a shift in business focus from designing and selling products only, to selling a system of products and services which are jointly capable of fulfilling specific client demands." Examples of product-service systems include solvent-leasing services, car-sharing services such as Zipcar, and

---

[2]The WEEE directive was enacted by the EU in 2003. Electronic equipment producers are required to take back their products at the end of their useful life. This directive is intended to encourage design for disassembly and remanufacture and also to support designs that can be repaired, reused, and recycled.

carpet-leasing systems. This concept can be applied to a range of products. In this scenario, manufacturers maintain ownership and responsibility, so they have an incentive to produce products that are durable, environmentally sound, and easily repairable.

How does this concept apply to the doll and toy industry? Dolls and toys can be designed to include service components that increase usability. For example, the American Girl company provides many "services": a doll hospital and doll hair grooming service, plus books, clothing, and accessories to enhance a child's enjoyment of the toy. These "services" can be problematic, however, as they also can encourage overconsumption. Another example of a product-service system for the toy industry is the Eureka Toy Library located in Alberton, South Africa. This library lends educational items and toys for children aged one through nine. To borrow items, families become library members for a small fee and may borrow toys for two weeks at a time; they can purchase a toy if the child wants to keep it. If a toy is broken, the member pays the repair or replacement cost (UNEP, 2002).

Product-service systems can be important components of sustainable product design in the toy industry. These systems can reduce resource use by designing for repairability, therefore extending the lifetime of the product. A toy library, as described above, also increases efficiency of resource use as parents can select an age-appropriate toy and then return it for other children to use, rather than purchasing and accumulating toys.

A HISTORY OF TERMINOLOGY: UNDERSTANDING THE CONCEPTS OF ECO DESIGN AND SUSTAINABLE DESIGN

In a 1991 report, the National Research Council (NRC) estimated that at least 70% of the cost of product development, manufacture, and use is determined at the design stage. Soon after, the U.S. Congress Office of Technology Assessment (OTA) released a report emphasizing that design is a critical determinant of competitiveness and also a key leverage point for addressing environmental impacts. OTA coined the term "green design" for a "design process in which environmental attributes are treated as design objectives, rather than as constraints" (U.S. Congress, 1992, p. 7). This report laid out two complementary goals for green design: prevent waste and improve materials management. In OTA's definition, preventing waste meant reducing weight, toxicity, and energy use and extending the service life of products. Improving materials management meant considering ways to remanufacture, recycle, compost, and recover energy.

The OTA report acknowledged tradeoffs between attributes. For example, some types of food packaging provide a longer shelf life and thus reduce food waste, but may not be recyclable because of the combination of materials used in the packaging. It also noted that a product could not be evaluated in isolation, but needed to be considered in the broader context of the production and consumption system in which it functioned. For example, computers contain many hazardous materials and it has proven challenging to design them as green products. A key OTA finding was that "green design is likely to have its largest impact in the context of changing the overall systems in which products are manufactured, used, and disposed, rather than in changing the composition of products per se" (U.S. Congress, 1992, p. 9).

The early 1990s was a fruitful time for the further development of "green design" which became known as "eco design" and "design for environment" (DFE). By the mid-1990s several textbooks and many journal articles had been written to explain this concept and provide tools and metrics. In 1996, Joseph Fiksel edited a book called *Design for Environment: Creating Eco-Efficient Products and Processes*. Fiksel defines DFE as "systematic consideration of design performance with respect to environmental, health, and safety objectives over the full product and process life cycle" (Fiksel, 1996, p. 3).

Like the OTA report, Fiksel (1996) describes DFE as providing a competitive advantage for firms and encouraging innovation. He frames DFE as the convergence of industry's efforts toward sustainable development and the reengineering of business systems to improve coordination across organizations; to him it provides a way to "achieve sustainability while seeking competitive advantage" (Fiksel, 1996, p. 5). In this broad framing, DFE encompasses occupational and consumer health and safety, and ecological integrity. DFE is the "design of safe and eco-efficient" products and may include many different approaches: material substitution, toxic use reduction, energy use reduction, life extension, and design for repairability and disassembly, recyclability, disposability, reusability, remanufacture, and energy recovery (p. 51).

Fiksel (1996) stresses that integrated product development is important in achieving "design for environment" goals. He defines this concept as "a process whereby all functional groups (e.g., engineering, manufacturing, marketing, etc.) that are involved in a product life cycle participate as a team in the early understanding and resolution of key product development issues including quality, manufacturability, reliability, maintainability, environment, and safety" (p. 66). This definition appears to broadly encompass sustainability; in practice, however, DFE tends to focus on maximizing the environmental attributes of products, and rarely considers the social impacts of a globalized production system.

A textbook by Thomas Graedel and Braden Allenby (1996), called *Design for Environment*, set DFE within the framework of industrial ecology. The authors describe "design for X" as a modern approach to industrial product design and note that "X" could be a focus on various aspects such as assembly, compliance, environment, manufacturability, reliability, or serviceability. Trade-offs may be required to achieve whatever variable is chosen for "X." This book provides practical recommendations on designing for energy efficiency and recycling, minimizing industrial process residues, and choosing materials. The authors make several valuable recommendations: choose abundant, nontoxic, nonregulated materials if possible; if toxic materials are required for manufacturing, try to generate them on-site rather than have them made elsewhere and shipped; choose natural rather than synthetic materials; design for minimum use of materials in products, processes, and services; and try to get most of the needed materials through recycling streams rather than through raw materials extraction. Thus they present a very practical approach to implementing DFE. However, their framework also fails to consider the social impacts of globalized production.

Since the early 1990s, the concept of eco design has also been gaining currency in Europe. In 1995, the Centre for Sustainable Design was established at the Surrey Institute of Art and Design at University College in Farnham, United Kingdom. This center, headed by Martin Charter, has held many conferences and workshops over the last decade and has served as a focal point for the development of both eco design and sustainable design concepts. Edwin Datschefski (1999), founder of BioThinking International in the United Kingdom, has developed an approach called "cyclic, solar, safe" to frame a new way of designing products that mimic natural systems. He cites the limits of eco-efficiency and urges manufacturers to create biocompatible products that will do no damage to the earth. A "cyclic" product is one whose materials can be recycled in a closed loop or are compostable or edible. A "solar" product is powered by photosynthesis, renewable energy or muscle power. A "safe" product is free from toxic releases at all stages. Although few products are currently biocompatible by Datschefski's definition, he provides a framework and design concepts for moving in this life-affirming direction.

William McDonough and Michael Braungart (2002), leading eco designers mentioned earlier, have developed a protocol called Cradle to Cradle Design, which echoes Datschefski's framework. Critiquing eco-efficiency for not addressing basic design flaws, they present three tenets of their vision for eco-effective design: waste equals food, use current solar income, and celebrate diversity. "Waste equals food" is intended to acknowledge that in natural systems, waste biodegrades and creates food for other organisms. This is a natural cycle of biological metabolism. McDonough and Braungart suggest that industrial systems should mimic this cycle by creating "technical metabolisms" that mirror biological systems. In their idealized vision, these would be closed-loop systems in which high-tech, benign, synthetic, and mineral resources circulate, so that no hazardous materials would interact with or harm the environment. The principle of "use current solar income" acknowledges the need for industrial systems to rely increasingly on renewable sources of energy. The third tenet—celebrate diversity—acknowledges that natural systems thrive on diversity and that solutions may vary with location. These three visionary tenets have been used to develop practical principles for "green engineering" such as using nonhazardous inputs, preventing waste, minimizing energy consumption and materials use, designing for targeted durability and necessary capacity, and minimizing materials diversity (McDonough, Braungart, Anastas, & Zimmerman, 2003).

In his book *Materials Matter*, Kenneth Geiser (2001) describes the unsustainable nature of our current systems of production and consumption as directly related to our choices of industrial materials. He traces the changes in industrial materials use over the last century and argues that a sustainable materials policy would emphasize detoxification and dematerialization as strategies to achieve sustainable production and consumption.

I have synthesized the core aspects of these frameworks into a set of six criteria for eco design as illustrated in Figure 2. These criteria form a starting point for developing a framework for sustainable product design.

A FRAMEWORK FOR
SUSTAINABLE PRODUCT DESIGN

Although the terms eco design and sustainable design are often used interchangeably, they are not synonymous. Eco design has its limits: a design that aims to maximize environmental attributes may not necessarily result in a product that is healthy in production and use, made in a way that is socially responsible, or economically viable. Eco design criteria fall short of encompassing the social and economic elements needed to create production and consumption systems that are truly sustainable.

In an economy in which design, production, and consumption occur in disparate locations, a range of decisions are made along the global supply chain about materials, chemicals, and the work environment that may impact a product's sustainability. The strategy to address environmental aspects separately from the

---

1. **Safe**: product is nontoxic in production and safe in use throughout its life cycle.

2. **Appropriately durable:** product can be repaired and reused. One-time use products are biodegradable.

3. **Efficient:** product uses energy, water, and materials efficiently during production and use. Waste is prevented/minimized throughout the product life cycle.

4. **Recyclable:** product can be recycled.

5. **Designed for disassembly:** product can be taken apart and remanufactured—this means materials diversity is minimized.

6. **Renewable resources and energy:** product uses renewable resources and energy in both production and use.

Figure 2. Eco design criteria.

health and social aspects of production has not proven to be a sound long-term approach, as these factors are intertwined. A product that is safe for consumers but presents significant hazards for those involved in its production is not a fully sustainable product. Similarly, a product that is polluting in its production and therefore adversely impacts the local community is not a fully sustainable product (even if this occurs far from where the product is consumed/used).

Sustainable product design considers who makes the product, going beyond the basic health and safety considerations that are encompassed in eco design criteria such as reducing the use of toxic materials. It considers working conditions throughout the supply chain as well as consumer safety and end-of-life issues. Workers often pay the price for economic pressures on manufacturers to cut corners to meet the demand for low-cost products. Even if toxic inputs are eliminated from a product design, workers may be subjected to unhealthy and inhumane working conditions, such as poor air quality, poor ergonomic design of work stations, involuntary overtime, and excessive pace.

For example, industrial designers Stuart Walker and Ed Dorsa (2001) have discussed how the "social well-being" component of sustainability relates to product design; they see a key role here for product designers. They argue that product designers can hinder progress toward sustainability if they do not consider the "form and quality" of employment needed to make the product. They note that "in the manufacturing sector the nature of work is critically related to the ways products are designed. It is therefore an industrial design issue" (p. 42).

Addressing a related issue, Robert Karasek (1992) has developed a "demand/control" model to predict job-related stress. According to this model, jobs that combine high demand with low control over the work process are particularly stressful; those with high demand and high "decision latitude" are less stressful. He uses the term "conducive production" to describe a healthy workplace design that is nonhierarchical, asks workers to take responsibility for coordinating their own jobs, and includes a broad recombination of skills (Karasek, 1999).

However, this integrated approach is not normally part of industrial design curricula. Designers are not generally taught to consider the implications for the work environment when they are designing a product. For products to be truly sustainable, industrial designers as well as other decision makers throughout the supply chain must begin to make these connections.

In their book *Design + Environment,* Helen Lewis and John Gertsakis (2001, p. 17) state that "sustainable design begins to address the bigger picture by considering collectively some of the harder questions, such as need, equity, ethics, social impact and total resource efficiency and thus the role of design in achieving inter-generational equity." Similarly, Ursula Tischner and Martin Charter (2001, pp. 119–121) note that "sustainable product design is more than eco design as it integrates social and ethical aspects of the product's life cycle alongside environmental and economic considerations—aiming for the so-called triple bottom line . . . sustainable product design means thinking through complex issues such as meeting the basic needs of the world's poor while reducing global inequalities and producing profitable solutions."

Tischner and Charter acknowledge the difficulty of integrating social and ethical aspects of product design into the product development process and note that the implementation of eco design has progressed much further than the social aspects of sustainable product design. They also note that it is difficult to train designers and product developers in the concept of sustainable product development.

The Natural Step's textbook, *Sustainability for Designers* (MacPherson, 2004), represents one of the first efforts to spell out sustainable product design and differentiate it from eco design. This manual asks designers to consider how their choice of materials has implications far beyond the product itself and challenges them to determine how to use far fewer resources in meeting human needs and desires. The textbook overlays the traditional product design process with The Natural Step Framework for implementing sustainability. In doing so, touchstones of design—function, efficiency, cost, timelessness, beauty, and elegance—are expanded to include principles of sustainability. This is a shift in intention for designers and requires asking a new set of questions during the product development process.

The Natural Step textbook frames three principles to guide the actions of designers as they realign their intentions with sustainability: dematerialize, substitute, and humanize. The first two principles are synonymous with eco design. To dematerialize, designers must significantly reduce material and energy usage in products. To substitute, designers must find alternatives to materials that are problematic from a sustainability perspective because they are toxic, persistent, bioaccumulative, or scarce.

The third principle, humanize, goes beyond eco design as it encompasses the social impacts of production and consumption. To humanize production, one must consider a range of issues. For example: do employees at each node of the product life cycle have safe and healthy working conditions? Does the design of work develop human capital or simply use it up? Do workers participate in decisions about the production process? Is the local community informed about the production process? Does the local community benefit from production? Are women and men are treated equally in the workplace? Is child labor forbidden? Do workers receive a living wage? Is the product fairly traded?

It remains a significant challenge to determine how to integrate broader issues of sustainability into the product design and development process. Building on the scholarship described above, I have created a conceptual framework for sustainable product design. Sustainable product design may be thought of as having five key elements, as illustrated in Figure 3. This figure acknowledges that these five elements of sustainability are interconnected and therefore all must be attended to in the creation of a sustainable product. Table 1 provides

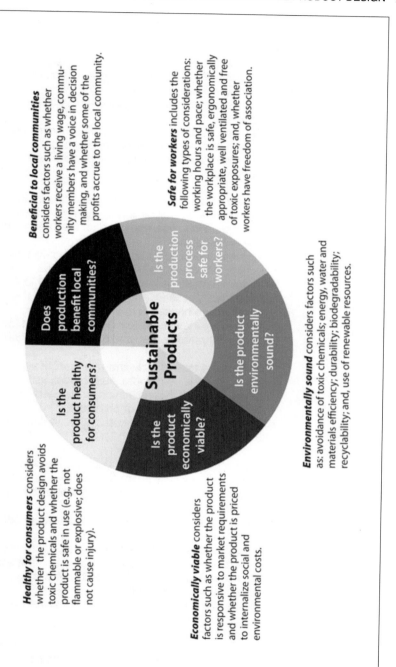

Figure 3. The five elements of sustainable product design.

Table 1. A Framework for Sustainable Product Design

Healthy for consumers A sustainable product is healthy for consumers. This means:	• It avoids chemicals that cause cancer or mutations, damage the reproductive, nervous, endocrine, or immune systems, are acutely toxic, or accumulate or persist in the environment. • It is safe in use—not flammable, explosive, or corrosive. • It is safe for children—does not cause lacerations, choking or strangling, burns/shocks, hearing damage, or eye injuries. It is developmentally appropriate.
Safe for workers A sustainable product is safe for workers. This means:	• Workplace is safe: clean, well lit, ventilated, with good air quality, well designed ergonomically, free of exposure to toxins, equipped for fire safety and other emergencies. • Workers receive adequate health and safety training. • Working hours and pace are not excessive. • Workers have some job control and input into production process. • If workers are housed in dormitories, the living quarters are clean and workers have sufficient food, access to potable water, and adequate sanitation facilities. • Workers are treated fairly and with respect and dignity; there is no corporal punishment, verbal abuse, coercion, discrimination, or harassment. • Child or forced labor is not permitted. • Workers have freedom of association and the right to collective bargaining.
Environmentally sound A sustainable product is environmentally sound. This means:	• Chemical and material inputs/outputs are not hazardous (see Healthy for Consumers above). • Product is energy, water, and materials efficient in production and use. • Waste is prevented and/or minimized throughout the product life cycle. • Product and packaging are durable as appropriate and are reused, repaired, recycled, or composted. • Product is designed for disassembly; it can be taken apart and remanufactured. • Renewable resources and energy are utilized in production and use. • Scarce resources are conserved and ecosystems are not damaged in extracting resources for production. • Critical habitats are preserved during extraction, production, and use.

Table 1. (Cont'd.)

Beneficial to local communities A sustainable product benefits the communities in which it is made. This means:	• Workers receive a living wage and can support their families without additional government assistance. • The work design is supportive to family life—e.g., families are not separated, and good-quality child-care is available for workers' children. • The work design promotes equity and fairness in the community—e.g., there is no age or gender discrimination. • Some of the firm's profits accrue to the local community to be used for public improvements (such as in education, health care). • The work design promotes community input and participation and the community is informed about production and labor practices.
Economically viable A sustainable product is economically viable for the firm/ organization. This means:	• The product is responsive to market requirements. • Innovation is encouraged to anticipate market needs. • The firm is stable in terms of ownership and philosophy. • The company reinvests in the facility to improve its capacity for further production. • Employees' skills are well utilized and their ideas and input are valued. • Communication is valued and encouraged among workers, management, community, and consumers. • The product is priced for economic viability and also aims to internalize costs so that its production can be environmentally sound and socially just.

the criteria for each of these five elements. I drew these criteria from several sources: existing eco design frameworks, voluntary codes to improve conditions for workers such as SA 8000, government requirements for toy safety, and principles of fair trade and sustainable community development.

Each element aims to address a different set of issues. The criteria for **healthy for consumers** consider a product's effect on the health and safety of those using it. For example, does the product avoid chemicals that cause cancer or mutations, that damage the reproductive, nervous, or endocrine systems, or that accumulate or persist in the environment? Is the toy flammable? Can a child choke on it? Is it developmentally appropriate? The criteria for **beneficial to local communities** include such factors as whether workers receive a living wage, whether community members have a voice in decision making, and whether some of the profits accrue to the local community. The criteria for **safe for workers** consider working conditions, such as hours and pace. Also, is the workplace safe, clean, well ventilated, and free of toxic exposures? Are workers free to associate? The criteria for **environmentally sound** consider the efficiency of energy, water, and materials use, the avoidance of toxic chemicals, the durability and recyclability of products, and the use of renewable resources. Finally, the criteria for **economically viable** weigh such factors as whether the product is responsive to market requirements and priced to internalize costs so that its production can be environmentally sound and socially just.

Sustainable product design is intimately linked with systems of sustainable production and consumption. The Lowell Center for Sustainable Production at the University of Massachusetts Lowell has defined sustainable production as "production systems that are non-polluting; conserving of energy and natural resources; economically efficient; safe and healthful for workers, neighbors, and consumers; and socially and creatively rewarding for employees" (Quinn, Kriebel, Geiser, & Moure-Eraso, 1998, p. 299).

Sustainable production efforts have focused primarily on improving workplace health and safety and reducing environmental impacts in manufacturing and in service sectors such as health care. Sustainable product design can enhance the implementation of sustainable production and consumption as it considers environmental, social, and economic factors throughout a product's life cycle, and aims to reduce impacts throughout the supply chain and during product consumption/use.

Sustainable product design cannot be implemented in the absence of systems of sustainable production and consumption. Figure 4 is intended to demonstrate the interconnectedness of sustainable design, production, and consumption. It illustrates how sustainable product design incorporates both traditional design elements (such as functionality, aesthetics, quality, cost, and safety for consumers) and the five elements of sustainable product design. The design process feeds into a cycle of sustainable production and consumption. In order for a sustainable design to be implemented, systems that support sustainable production and consumption must be operational. These include government, corporate, and citizen-based strategies such as regulations to phase out toxic chemicals, economic incentives for sustainable product development, institutional purchasing policies that specify a preference for sustainable products, detailed product labeling, transparent and effective codes of conduct and standards, and increased public pressure for humane working conditions and comprehensive environmental management. I discuss these linkages further in chapter 8.

I used this framework for sustainable product design as an organizing tool in conducting qualitative research on doll making in different parts of the world. These case studies are described in chapters 4 through 6. In some cases, the data required to make a comprehensive assessment were

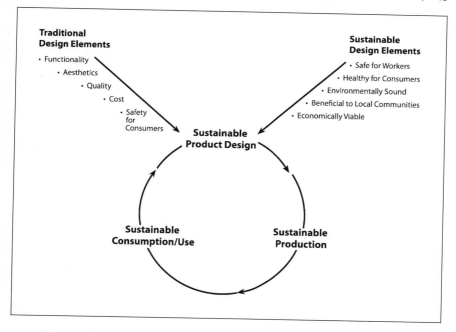

Figure 4. Linking sustainable product design, sustainable production, and sustainable consumption.

lacking.[3] Still, these elements proved very useful as a conceptual framework for envisioning sustainable product design and considering strengths and weaknesses of products in light of these five key factors. In chapter 7, I discuss the themes that emerged from my analysis.

[3]For example, I was not able to collect data on energy efficiency, nor was I able to travel to China and observe working/living conditions of workers in Chinese toy factories.

CHAPTER 4

The American Girl Company

The success story of the American Girl company includes a brilliant design and marketing plan created by Pleasant Rowland, which was eventually matched with a global production and consumption system effectively utilized by Mattel, the world's largest toy company. In this chapter I tell the story of the American Girl doll, describing its design, marketing strategy, and psychology. I take readers behind the scenes to a typical doll-making factory in China to reveal the conditions under which these dolls are made. I also review the audits of Mattel's vendor factories between 2002 through 2006 to better understand the work environment and analyze the changes that have been made as a result of these inspections.

Pleasant Rowland created the American Girl doll in 1985. Rowland, then in her mid-40s, had no formal business training but she did have a wide range of professional experience as an elementary school teacher, author of children's reading textbooks, and publisher of a small magazine. In 1984 she visited colonial Williamsburg, Virginia, and was impressed with its effectiveness in creating "living history." She pondered how this concept could be used to bring history alive for children. Later that year she was searching for dolls as Christmas gifts for her nieces, then aged 8 and 10, and was disappointed at the limited choices available. She could select either a Cabbage Patch doll or a Barbie, but neither design met her needs or desires. Rowland described her experience, "Here I was, in a generation of women at the forefront of redefining women's roles yet our daughters were playing with dolls that celebrated being a teen queen or a mommy. I knew I couldn't be the only woman in America who was unhappy with these Christmas choices" (Rowland & Sloane, 2002, para. 4).

Out of these experiences came her idea to create a series of books about 9-year-old girls at different times in history, accompanied by a doll, clothes, and accessories that were historically accurate. With $1 million in royalties from her textbooks, Rowland did not need to look for start-up funds. Although the concept was initially panned by a focus group of mothers, when they saw the actual doll and book they were sold on the idea and by 1986 the Pleasant Company was up and running. In the first year of production, sales were $1.7 million. Only

5 years later, in 1991, sales were $77 million, rising to $300 million by 1996 and $380 million by 2004 (Arndorfer, 2005; Rowland & Sloane, 2002). As of January 2008, over 13 million American Girl dolls and 117 million American Girl books have been purchased.[1]

In 1998, Mattel bought the Pleasant Company for $700 million (Rowland & Sloane, 2002). Rowland was a vice president of Mattel until 2000, when she moved on to other opportunities. For Mattel, this purchase was a strategic acquisition of a successful product in a niche market that the company had not yet tapped, especially at a time when Barbie sales were declining. Some observers, however, saw the irony when a product once marketed as an "anti-Barbie" was purchased by Barbie's makers. Pleasant Rowland responded to her critics as follows: "I felt a genuine connection to Jill Barad [then CEO of Mattel], the woman who built Barbie. The ironies did not escape me . . . but I saw in Jill a blend of passion, perfectionism, and perseverance with real business savvy" (Rowland & Sloane, 2002, para. 16).

What is responsible for the phenomenal success of this doll? The American Girl company's mission is simply "to celebrate girls." The company tapped into an unexploited preteen demographic (ages 8–12) and has cleverly marketed this product to both parents and children, offering not only dolls, but also books, clothing for dolls and girls, accessories, and a unique retail experience for mothers and daughters.

PRODUCT DESIGN

We give girls chocolate cake with vitamins. Our books are exciting, our magazine is fun, and the dolls and accessories are pretty. But more important, they give young girls a sense of self and an understanding of where they came from and who they are today. (Pleasant T. Rowland, cited in Heer-Forsberg, 2005, retrieved 2006, para. 16)

The product line includes 13 dolls encompassing historical periods from 1764 to 1974; they include a Nez Perce Indian girl, two colonial girls, a "Hispanic" girl in New Mexico, a pioneer girl, a fugitive slave girl, a wealthy orphan living in New York at the turn of the 20th century, a poor Irish immigrant girl of this same time period, a girl growing up in the Depression, two girls growing up during World War II, and two girls (one Chinese American) living in San Francisco in the 1970s. The dolls are 18 inches high. Their torsos are soft, made of cloth; their heads, arms, and legs are hard vinyl. Their eyes are plastic and their hair is made of a synthetic material. Each doll is dressed in an outfit that is historically

---

[1] See www.americangirl.com/corp/media/fastfacts.html

accurate and is packaged with a book that begins to tell her story. Photos and a description of each doll can be found on the American Girl Web site.[2]

It is these books that differentiate these dolls from others on the market. The story of each American Girl is told in a six-book series. The series is formulaic, yet appealing, especially to elementary school-aged girls who enjoy reading about girl heroines. The American Girl is introduced in the first book, along with family members and significant friends. The story that unfolds in the next five books requires the American Girl to be brave, resourceful, loyal to her family, and kind to others. By the sixth book the character has matured and learned some important life lessons. The books have been rightly criticized for their individualist approach and simplification of historical context, but they do provide a strong message of empowerment for girls in the 9 to 12 age range (Acosta-Alzuru & Roushanzamir, 2003). Additional clothes and accessories are designed to help the doll owner follow the story line for her doll. For example, each doll has a special Christmas dress, and historically accurate accessories such as bedroom furniture, tables, and chairs, most with price tags of $100 or more.

Although Pleasant Rowland conceived of the American Girl doll as a way to bring history alive, the company has expanded its product offerings far beyond the historical dolls. In 1995, the company added a doll line called American Girls of Today (now known as "just like you") that are the same size and made of the same materials as the historical dolls. Consumers may choose from 23 options of hair, eye, and skin color for a doll that looks "just" like them. This doll comes with a blank book of questions, and the owner can create her own story. The many accessories available for the "modern" American Girl dolls mirror preteen life today; they include soccer and gymnastics outfits, cell phones, and drum sets. To appeal to 3–7 year olds, "Bitty Baby" was introduced, also available in various skin tones. The publishing arm of American Girl has also grown. In addition to offering new stories that feature the historical American Girl characters, the company began a line of advice and activity books for girls. One of the most popular, *The Care and Keeping of You: Body Book for Girls* has sold more than 2 million copies since 1998.[3]

Pleasant Rowland designed a high-quality doll to be treasured. The high cost of these dolls ($87) means that they are likely to be passed on to siblings or friends or saved for grandchildren rather than thrown away. The company's doll hospital is an integral part of its customer service and also encourages additional consumption. As described on the American Girl Web site, "Life happens. That's why there's the American Girl Doll Hospital, for everything from a general cleaning to "major surgery." Doll doctors can make an American Girl as

---

[2] See http://www.americangirl.com/
[3] See www.americangirl.com/corp/media/fastfacts.htm

good as new and send her back ready to be loved for a lifetime."[4] If a limb falls off, the doll can be repaired for $24. For the same price, dolls may also be sent to the "hospital" for a "wellness" visit where their "skin" will be cleaned and their hair brushed, and they will receive a hospital gown and certificate. If desired, the doll can be returned in a wheelchair for $30. The dolls are cleaned and repaired, and return with hospital accessories that can be incorporated into imaginative play.

MARKETING STRATEGY AND PSYCHOLOGY

> Once we got the product right, the marketing had to have some magic in it. It was clear to me that American Girl was a thinking girl's product line, one that would not sell at Toys "R" Us. It wasn't meant to blare from the shelves on its packaging or visual appeal alone. It had a more important message— one that had to be delivered in a softer voice. A 30-second commercial couldn't do the job. (Rowland & Sloane, 2002, para. 10)

Rowland decided to use direct mail advertising to sell her product. She got advice from Lands End, a clothing company also based in Wisconsin, and prepared her first mailing of 500,000 catalogs in 1986 (Rowland & Sloane, 2002). The direct mail approach allowed Rowland to explain her product in more depth and include many photos of dolls and their accessories. Through these catalogs and word of mouth, sales grew rapidly. In 1997, the company created a Web site and an online store.

As the final element in her business plan, Rowland created a unique retail store for American Girl products, based on a special "mother-daughter" day she remembers spending with her mother in the 1950s. In November 1998, American Girl Place in Chicago opened to great fanfare. Billed as an "entertainment" or "experiential" retail site, the complex includes a café (where American Girl dolls are seated and welcomed with their own doll-sized plates and cups), a theater with a theatrical revue of historical American Girl themes, a doll hair salon, a "museum" with dioramas from the different historical periods represented by the dolls, and, of course, retail shops. Grossing $40 million a year, this store has become one of Chicago's most popular tourist attractions (Heer-Forsberg, 2005). An American Girl place in New York City (on Fifth Avenue across from Rockefeller Center) opened in 2003, followed by one in Los Angeles in April 2006. In late 2007, the company launched a new concept called the American Girl Boutique and Bistro. In both Atlanta and Dallas, these locations provide party rooms for American-Girl-themed birthday parties and also offer a casual restaurant, doll salon, and retail shopping. As of May 2009, 23 million people have visited these stores.[5]

[4]See http://store.americangirl.com/agshop/static/dollHospital.jsf
[5]See www.americangirl.com/corp/media/fastfacts.html

Other marketing devices include *American Girl* magazine, which debuted in 1992; its circulation of 620,000 makes it one of the most popular children's magazines in the United States.[6] Described as an "age appropriate, advertising-free publication designed to affirm self-esteem, celebrate achievements, and foster creativity in today's girls," the magazine contains stories and advice for girls aged 7 to 12 (Heer-Forsberg, 2005, para. 9). It is published six times per year; each issue generates 10,000 pieces of mail from readers.[7] American Girl also has a very popular Web site; each year 22 million girls visit its "fun for girls" section of games and activities. According to company statistics, 95% of girls in the United States aged 7 to 12 are familiar with American Girl dolls.[8] Clearly these marketing strategies have been highly effective.

> Parents know "the American Girl products are something they can really do for their daughters vs. just another thing they can get." (Arndorfer, 2005, para. 7)

The American Girl doll is marketed brilliantly to parents as well as children. The company's only ad campaign to date, "Save Girlhood," debuted in the fall of 2005. Part of the ad copy read: ". . . from every angle, today's girls are bombarded by influences pushing them toward womanhood at too early an age—at the expense of their innocence, their playfulness, their imagination (Cabot, 2005, para. 3). The implication is that by buying American Girl dolls for their daughters, parents can hold the adult world at bay. Parents of all backgrounds and political persuasions are concerned that the electronic media force children to grow up too fast. Thus a traditional toy, like this doll, is attractive. For the company, any tactic that extends the age range of children who play with these dolls can provide a financial advantage.

The American Girl company differentiates itself from other toy companies by associating its merchandise with "American" values such as friendship, community, and education (Acosta-Alzuru & Roushanzamir, 2003). In doing so, it constructs its image as a company that is motivated by the desire to improve the well-being of girls rather than being driven by the profit motive (Acosta-Alzuru & Roushanzamir, 2003). But consumerism is clearly not an influence from which they protect girls. On the contrary, the company's magazines, catalogs, web sites, and stores are highly effective in teaching these preteen girls about their place in mass consumption. The high-quality dolls are designed to be treasured and cherished. But the monthly catalogs remind children relentlessly that one doll is not enough and that they need additional accessories to play with them successfully.

---

[6] See www.americangirl.com/corp/media/fastfacts.html
[7] See www.americangirl.com/corp/media/fastfacts.html
[8] See www.americangirl.com/corp/media/fastfacts.html

Because these dolls and their accoutrements have become play date "currency" for affluent children, some girls experience intense pressure to keep up with peers by having the same number of dolls and a similar volume of accessories. These girls become intensely focused on acquiring multiple dolls and clothes to achieve status in their social relationships with their peers. This behavior can set the stage for a pattern of overconsumption that carries through to adulthood (Schor, 2005).

Both feminist and conservative mothers find the American Girl doll appealing for their daughters, but for somewhat different reasons. Feminists may be seeking alternatives to the Barbie and Bratz[9] style of fashion dolls and traditionalists may be drawn to the wholesomeness and patriotism that the American Girl doll represents. Rowland is described as holding fast to her "Midwestern morals" in the company's efforts "to do right by little girls" (Rowland & Sloane, 2002, para. 2).

But this diverse community of consumers is rather fragile, as became clear in a controversy that erupted in the fall of 2005. In August, American Girl had launched the "I Can" campaign, encouraging girls to wear an "I CAN" bracelet and sign the American Girl "I CAN" Promise: I can be myself, follow my dreams, and always do my best. I can reach for the stars, lend a hand to others, and be a good friend. I can make a difference! I promise to try (American Girl Company press release, August 22, 2005). Proceeds were to go to Girls, Inc., a national nonprofit organization supporting programs for underprivileged girls. On the surface, this was an innocuous campaign. However, because Girls, Inc. supports reproductive freedom, contraception, and gay rights, conservative groups such as the American Family Association began an e-mail campaign calling on members to write letters and boycott the company's products.[10] The American Girl company continued its financial support of Girls, Inc. through December 2005, but clarified that its donations to Girls, Inc. were earmarked for programs in math, science, athletics, and leadership (American Girl Company press release, December 26, 2005).

PROVIDING JOBS AND PHILANTHROPY

While our award-winning product lines and outstanding customer service are sure to catch your attention, we feel it's the opportunity to interact with dynamic, creative people that makes for a great place to work. An atmosphere

[9]Bratz Dolls were introduced in 2001 by MGA Entertainment as an updated fashion doll. The Bratz byline is "the only girls with a passion for fashion!" See www.bratz.com

[10] At least one business has created a "Christian" alternative to the American Girl doll. A company called Life of Faith has launched a line of 18-inch vinyl dolls that are "role models that imagine and experience a lifestyle of faith." The dolls come with "faith-based historical novels" that tell their life story. See http://www.alof.com

of genuine caring about our products, customers and each other, and our ability to turn dreams and ideas into reality make for a rewarding career at American Girl.[11]

The American Girl Company has its corporate headquarters in Middleton, Wisconsin, just outside of Madison. The company's facilities also include warehouse and distribution sites in Wilmot and DeForest, Wisconsin, and in Edison, New Jersey, and an outlet store in Oshkosh, Wisconsin, along with three retail stores and the two Boutique and Bistro locations described earlier. The company employs approximately 1800 people throughout the year, adding more than 4700 employees during the pre-holiday season.[12] Mattel's Web site describes Middleton, Wisconsin, as "one of the best cities in the country to live, work, play, and raise a family." Also described are some of the special benefits of working at the company: Friday half days as the corporate office closes at 1 P.M., a summer company picnic, an on-site café, and fourth-quarter festivities to help keep employees energized during the peak season.[13]

The company has a solid record of corporate philanthropy to children's charities in the United States. These efforts also promote the American Girl brand. For example, for nonprofit organizations, the company provides an American Girl fashion show as a unique fundraising opportunity.[14]

The company participates in United Way and the Special Olympics and donates dolls and books to schools and libraries for auction and raffle fundraisers. It also donates returned merchandise and seconds to the Madison Children's Museum, where these products are sold at an annual benefit sale, which has raised over $11 million. A percentage of these proceeds is returned to the company and redistributed through the American Girl Fund for Children, which provides local grants to "enhance children's education in the arts and environment." For example, this program has funded the Aldo Leopold Nature Center and Nature Net, "a collaborative consortium of natural sites in southern Wisconsin dedicated to environmental education of elementary school children."[15]

The creator of the American Girl doll, Pleasant T. Rowland, and her husband, businessman W. Jerome Frautschi are known as generous philanthropists in their home community of Madison. After she retired from Mattel, Rowland set up the Pleasant T. Rowland Foundation, known as one of the top 50 Wisconsin

[11] From Mattel's Web site: http://www.mattel.com/careers/ca_work_madis.asp
[12] See http://www.americangirl.com/corp/history.html
[13] See http://www.mattel.com/careers/ca_work_madis.asp
[14] http://www.americangirl.com/corp/philanthropy.html
[15] http://www.americangirl.com/corp/philanthropy.html

foundations in grant giving.[16] Rowland describes her philanthropic approach as follows: "I have sought projects that build, enrich, and beautify community in places that matter to me, for the enjoyment of those that live here today and for those in generations to come. I deeply believe that we are all profoundly impacted by our surroundings. If the places we live and work in are cared for we will feel cared for; and, if we feel cared for, we will take better care of each other" (Edmondson, 2002, para. 32).

In the same year she sold her company to Mattel for $700 million, her husband gave a gift of $50 million to develop a cultural arts district in downtown Madison. By the end of phase one of construction, he had contributed over $200 million to this effort.[17] In addition, the Pleasant T. Rowland Foundation contributed significantly toward the purchase and maintenance of a concert organ in Madison's new concert hall.

The Pleasant T. Rowland Foundation has also made generous grants beyond the city of Madison, including $5 million to the Chicago Botanic Garden to create a new garden and visitors' area and a $500,000 scholarship grant to the Pacific Crest Outward Bound School in Portland, Oregon, "to ensure that young women will always have the opportunity to take on the challenge and adventure of an Outward Bound course."[18]

One of Rowland's more controversial philanthropic ventures is in Aurora, New York, home of her alma mater, Wells College. In the early 2000s, the Pleasant T. Rowland Foundation purchased almost all of the commercial property in town and set up the Aurora Foundation, with Rowland controlling 51% of the Foundation and Wells College controlling 49%. At first, many residents were hopeful about the potential for revitalizing their community, but some were concerned that too much decision-making power was concentrated in Rowland's hands (Miller, 2001). Between 2001 and 2006, Rowland provided funds for and oversaw the renovation of several properties, including a historic inn and a restaurant, causing the community to gentrify rapidly. Proponents appreciate the new and thriving businesses in town, but many oppose the changes, particularly because Rowland decided to gut the interior of some historic buildings. In June 2006, she gave Wells College control of the businesses and buildings she had restored, signaling an end to her efforts in Aurora ("No Storybook Ending," 2007).

From the descriptions above, the American Girl headquarters in Madison appears to be a very appealing place to work. In addition, the company and

[16] http://foundationcenter.org/findfunders/statistics/pdf/03_fund_geo/2005/50_found_states/f_wi_05.pdf

[17] http://www.overturecenter.com/mission.htm

[18] See http://www.women-philanthropy.umich.edu/donors/donors_nz.html#R and http://www.gatesfoundation.org/UnitedStates/PacificNorthwest/Announcements/Announce-187.htm

Rowland herself have been very generous in sharing profits with the local community and with other places in the United States in which they have a personal stake. But do these working conditions and financial munificence carry over to the places far from Wisconsin where the doll is actually produced: in factories in Southern China?

THE PRODUCTION PROCESS IN A TYPICAL CHINESE DOLL-MAKING FACTORY

The American Girl company, like most successful toy companies, has taken advantage of the low labor costs and large economies of scale to be found by locating production in factories in southern China. American Girl dolls were originally produced in Germany, with accessories made in China and some doll clothing made in Hungary. In the early 1990s, the company relocated its manufacturing from Europe to factories in China. It appears that the original decision to produce dolls in Germany was serendipitous. Rowland describes how she asked a friend to find a "cute" doll at Marshall Fields in Chicago. This doll was made by the Götz factory in Rodental, West Germany. Rowland contacted the company and began a business relationship (Rowland & Sloane, 2002).

I did not have the opportunity to visit Mattel's factories in China where American Girl dolls are made, and so cannot provide a first-hand description of the production process for these dolls. The following general description of assembly-line production of vinyl dolls is likely to be similar to the actual production process for the American Girl doll.

The typical production process for a mass-produced plastic doll includes the following steps. First, a designer draws the doll. Next, a sculptor makes clay models of the doll parts. From these three dimensional models, rubber molds are produced. The next step is to make wax models from the rubber mold. These wax models are sanded and cleaned until they are considered ready to make permanent molds for mass production. The sturdy metal production molds, made at specialized factories, allow for the dolls to be mass-produced.

At the doll-making factory, workers attach the production molds to injection molding machines and pour liquid vinyl into them. The molds are then heated to a high temperature and spun so that the vinyl will coat the inside of the mold evenly. The molds are then cooled and the vinyl parts removed. Next, parts are inspected, faces are decorated, and plastic eyes are inserted. Wigs are glued on or rooted hair is sewn directly on to the head. Next, the dolls are assembled. The head, arms, and legs may be hand-sewn to a fabric body or attached to a plastic body. Finally, the doll is dressed and hair is groomed. Tags are attached after a final inspection (Young, 1992, pp. 44–50).

WORKING CONDITIONS AND ENVIRONMENTAL ISSUES
IN MATTEL'S CHINESE FACTORIES

What are the working conditions in Mattel's Chinese toy factories where the American Girl doll is produced? The excerpts below, from reports generated by corporate and non-governmental sources, include detailed descriptions and provide a picture of typical conditions in Chinese toy factories. Much of the information in this section comes from the International Center for Corporate Accountability (ICCA) audit reports. As described in chapter 2, the ICCA is a nonprofit organization that Mattel funds to audit working conditions at its own and vendor factories around the world.

In 1997, the ICCA, working with Mattel, developed a set of Global Manufacturing Principles (GMP) to lay out clear expectations for factory managers. The GMP specify detailed standards for 11 principles: management systems, wages and working hours, age requirements, forced labor, discrimination, freedom of expression and association, living conditions, workplace safety, health, emergency planning, and environmental protection. The ICCA conducts audits to determine compliance with the GMP. In this section, I review the results of ICCA's audits of Mattel's vendor plants in China conducted in 2002, 2003, and 2005 and follow-up audits conducted in 2004 and 2005 (ICCA, January and December 2004; ICCA, 2006a, 2006b).

In addition, several human rights advocacy organizations have investigated working conditions and published reports of their findings, which also provided valuable information for this chapter. These organizations include the National Labor Committee (NLC) and China Labor Watch based in New York City; Swedwatch based in Årsta, Sweden; and the Hong Kong Christian Industrial Committee (HKCIC) and the Asia Monitor Resource Center based in Hong Kong. These reports provide evidence that some factories keep two sets of books and pay bonuses to workers if they tell auditors that they work only 8 hours per day, 6 days per week (Hong Kong Christian Industrial Committee [HKCIC], 2001).

Activist groups acknowledge that Mattel is one of the best toy companies in terms of improving health and safety, limiting work hours, and ensuring fair pay (Goldman, 2004). Mattel has built its own factories in China, in which conditions are far better than the typical Chinese-owned factory. One description of a Mattel-owned factory, published in the *Los Angeles Times* in 2004, described the factory as follows: "The factory floor at Mattel Die-Cast China in Guanyao is bright and airy. Instead of the usual snaking assembly line, where workers perform the same task over and over and over, many MDC employees move around to different stations, often making an entire toy themselves; this helps eliminate painful repetitive-stress injuries. MDC's residence halls are more modern and nicer than dorms at top Chinese universities. In their off hours, workers crowd into the television rooms on each floor or play badminton on outdoor courts. Some head to the gym or to computer centers to practice lessons they learn in free classes offered on site. The quality of life here is written on the face of nearly every MDC worker: They smile, a rare expression at other plants" (Goldman, 2004, p. 4).

Unfortunately, this description of a Mattel-owned factory is the exception rather than the rule. Reports, from both ICCA and advocacy groups, paint a disturbing picture of conditions in Chinese-owned toy factories that are suppliers for Mattel and other companies, even if they differ somewhat in the details, such as the number of overtime hours employees actually work.[19] Taken together, these reports provide a vivid picture of the daily hardships faced by the majority of Chinese toy workers.

To begin, here are the voices of two toy workers at a typical Chinese-owned factory that manufactures toys for Mattel and other toy companies:

> Every day we work in temperatures that can be over 100 degrees. The molding machines are noisy and hot. The air is filled with a strong chemical smell. I have to repeat the same motions, over and over, open the machine, put in the plastic, press the machine, take out the plastic. . . . A lot of us can't stand the heat, the smell and the noise, and some of us faint. (NLC, 2002, p. 16)

> We work long overtime hours like dogs. It's after midnight when we get back to the dormitory. And it makes you even more tired when you see the long line at the bathroom. By the time I go to bed, it's already 2 A.M. and at 8 A.M. the next day, I am already at my workplace. It's the same every day. It's very exhausting. (NLC, 2002, p. 16)

Mattel outsources about half of its production to 40 vendors in China (ICCA, January 2004). Providing a snapshot of life inside a typical toy factory is the ICCA's 2002/2003 audit of 12 of Mattel's vendor factories; there are approximately 53,000 workers in these 12 factories, representing approximately 43% of the workforce employed by Mattel's vendors in China (ICCA, January 2004, p. 3).[20]

A key audit finding was excessive work hours. The auditors note that "most of the vendors were scheduling work hours that were in excess of the 60 hr/week limit stipulated in the GMP" (p. 12). In addition, "a large part of overtime is mandatory and built into the workers' employment expectations where the normal work week is described as 60 or 66 hours . . . the problem of excessive overtime is generally related to peak production periods when a workweek can easily extend to 72 hours and beyond" (p. 17). The auditors also noted

---

[19] The NGO reports note that workers may work as many as 120 hours per week with no days off, whereas the ICCA's follow-up audit states that these vendor factories are holding to a policy of 72 hours per week maximum (ICCA, December 2004; NLC, 2002).

[20] All information in this section is drawn from the ICCA report of January 2004.

"a particularly serious noncompliance of voluntary overtime policy . . . the entire workforce of 4600 workers was asked to work on a national holiday" (p. 17).

Another problem area described was denial of paid leave. Under Chinese labor law, workers receive five days of paid leave once they complete a year's service. The auditors noted that "many vendors observe the law . . . [but] others have denied their workers this benefit . . . in other cases, vendors create a policy whereby workers are paid for annual leave benefits only if they ask for it, and workers who are unaware of this policy forego their leave benefits" (p. 21). The report also noted problems with the treatment of pregnant workers, as some vendors refuse to hire them and others would fire workers found to be pregnant (p. 21).

The ICCA audits include a health, safety, and environment inspection. In all the factories audited, effective environmental management systems were lacking. Emergency equipment was poorly maintained and difficult to retrieve in seven of twelve plants. Auditors also noted that "in four other plants, emergency evacuation exits were blocked by boxes of stored materials" (pp. 38–39).

Inadequate ventilation and a lack of attention to industrial hygiene is a serious problem in all the factories that were inspected. Auditors note that almost all plants had ventilation systems that did not work properly or were not installed (p. 36). "A critical issue . . . is improper and insufficient ventilation and air filtration creating potential health hazards for workers especially in the areas of Tampo printing and soldering.[21] In the former case, exhaust systems are generally poorly maintained. In the later case, workers doing the soldering are given facemasks while workers sitting across the same assembly line are not wearing facemasks. . . . Workers in all plants, with the exception of Plant #2, complained of strong chemical odor at their workstations and of inadequate exhaust or ventilation systems . . . workers complained about uncomfortable level of indoor temperature" (p. 35).

Workers are supposed to be given personal protective equipment (PPE) but floor-level supervisors generally did not supervise or enforce PPE usage. Also, workers were "less inclined to use the PPE" when the temperatures were too high in the work area (p. 35). Because of inadequate ventilation and lack of personal protective equipment, workers are exposed to unhealthy levels of toxins in the production process such as heavy metals (lead, cadmium), solvents, plasticizers, glues, and dyes. Some of these chemicals, such as phthalates, may disrupt the endocrine system, and so are particularly harmful if exposure occurs during the key reproductive period of 18–30 years, the age of most Chinese factory workers.

Another problem is the storage of toxics. "Most plants routinely left some chemical containers without lids and stored them in improper areas without Material Safety Data Sheets." Often these areas did not have "sufficient ventilation

---

[21] Tampo printing, a process commonly used to print on plastic, involves the use of a silicone rubber printing pad.

or exhaust systems." The auditors commented that "plant management in general underestimate the health-related risks to their workers and the environment" (p. 36).

Auditors also observed improper treatment of wastewater; they noted that "most plants also lacked proper monitoring systems for wastewater and industrial waste disposal (p. 36). And, "similar to wastewater treatment, most plants seemed to pay little attention to underground leakage and soil contamination" (p. 37).

After the first audit of vendor factories was completed in 2004, Mattel's internal auditors analyzed the findings and worked with factory management to correct problems. Mattel worked with vendors to create management systems that would "greatly reduce, if not completely eliminate, occurrence of similar problems in the future" (ICCA, December 2004, p. 6). Mattel then presented the ICCA with a detailed report illustrating the changes that it had implemented. The ICCA responded that "a detailed analysis of the report provided ICCA with a large measure of assurance that most of the changes recommended had indeed been made and that no further action was needed" (ICCA, December 2004, p. 7).[22]

After the initial audit, Mattel revised its GMP standard upward to allow a maximum of 72 hours a week (40 regular and 32 overtime) during peak periods for 17 weeks per year. For the remaining 35 weeks, the maximum hours cannot exceed 60 per week. Also, workers cannot work more than 13 consecutive days without a rest day. This revision was "an attempt to find a middle ground whereby vendors could operate their plants and also provide workers with greater opportunities to earn additional overtime wages during peak production periods" (p. 11). Essentially, this revision gave factory managers more flexibility to schedule overtime. In 2004, Mattel informed the ICCA that it was terminating its relationship with Plant #7 after the original audit because of numerous violations related to payment of wages, excessive overtime, and inadequate record keeping. However, this termination did not occur. Mattel has continued its contract with this plant for "business reasons" (p. 8).

In 2004, the ICCA conducted a follow-up audit of seven of the twelve plants to verify that compliance was indeed adequate. The follow-up audit seemed to indicate progress. For example, it reported progress on industrial hygiene: "with minor exceptions, exceptional progress has been made in areas of housekeeping, proper use of PPE, electrical and mechanical equipment maintenance, grounds keeping, and in some instances proper ventilation . . . should vendors maintain their current level of effort toward improving physical facilities, ICCA believes that the vast majority of existing problems will be eliminated in the foreseeable future" (p. 17).

---

[22] All information in this section is drawn from the ICCA report of December 2004.

Progress also seemed clear on environmental management: "with the exception of one plant, monitoring applications for air emissions, wastewater and boundary noise permits have also been submitted to the Environmental Protection Bureau . . . exceptional progress has been made in clearing up external environmental issues and the efforts should continue until all major objectionable problem areas have been eliminated" (p. 18).

The audit also noted progress on work hours. Except for two plants, all the others "were in full compliance with the revised standard for work hours." Yet it noted that "some vendors were also suspected of keeping double sets of books and thereby apparently meeting the GMP standards while in practice violating them" (pp. 10, 13). It also noted, with "considerable alarm," another problem in the revised standard: that it "leaves additional room for manipulating GMP standards through creative interpretation of terms like "extraordinary situation" (p. 14).

In June 2006, the ICCA released audit results for seven additional facilities that are major suppliers for Mattel in China (ICCA, 2006b). In a press release, the ICCA reported that the minimum age of 16 was being enforced, that plants were in compliance with record-keeping and payment of the legally mandated minimum wage, and that almost all facilities "provided voluntary use of safe and clean dormitories and most had good food service available" (ICCA, 2006c, pp. 1–2). However, the report found "some inadequacies pertaining to environmental issues, including disposal of wastewater and poor ventilation . . . improvements needed with safety training and use of personal protective equipment" (ICCA, 2006c, p. 2). And, most facilities "exceeded the maximum overtime hours limits for peak production periods" (ICCA, 2006c, p. 2).

It is striking that all of the vendors audited in 2005 continue to violate Mattel's Global Manufacturing Principles in regard to overtime hours. According to the audit report: "rather than complying with expanded overtime limits, the new standard has become the minimum starting point . . . the current situation is untenable and Mattel needs to find a better answer to this problem" (ICCA, 2006b, p. 19).

The audit report also points out other ongoing problems. For example, permit systems that regulate workers' access to drinking water and rest rooms result in employees waiting an uncomfortably long time. At one plant workers were required to get a permit from their line leader to use the rest room, with 4 permits allowed per 50 workers. Many workers (95% at one plant) are not familiar with the Global Manufacturing Principles and others are confused about their pay stubs and overtime hours. Medical facilities are inadequate at factories with thousands of workers. Overall, factories have a mixed record regarding health, safety, and environmental issues. Some of the facilities are modern and have updated equipment, whereas others have failing infrastructure. Many workers complain of excessive noise and high temperatures, and the audit report notes that inadequate exhaust systems result in workers' inhalation of flux fumes and strong solvent and paint odors (ICCA, 2006b).

It is sobering to review this report and compare it to earlier audit results. Mattel is to be admired for creating a detailed set of principles and audit tools, for independently verifying and posting the reports on the Internet, and for linking compliance with GMP with performance.[23] Mattel does seem to have addressed some of the issues we can think of as "low hanging fruit," such as providing hot water in dormitories and updating equipment. Also, child labor is a "zero tolerance" area and the audits have not found any noncompliance in this arena, although a report prepared by China Labor Watch states that workers under age 16 "present fake ID cards or borrow others' cards to enter into employment" (China Labor Watch, 2005, p. 8).

However, the process of change is painfully slow and a detailed reading of these reports reveals tinkering at the edges of a broken system, rather than significant change toward humane working conditions. In particular, Mattel has not succeeded in solving the problem of excessive overtime hours. This is clearly a system-wide problem. Workers receive meager salaries and in general are not provided with training and development of their human capital so that they can advance in life. Also, most workers continue to face at least one of the following unsafe conditions: lack of or inadequate personal protective equipment, lack of training in handling hazardous materials, poor ventilation, or fire exits blocked by supplies. In addition, although discrimination and freedom of expression and association are included as GMP principles, it is questionable whether employees can speak openly on these topics and whether there is real accountability for factory managers to make improvements in these areas.

Although Mattel believes that its efforts at implementing the GMP are helping to improve conditions throughout toy factories in China, clearly a long road lies ahead. As is true of most manufacturing that occurs far from the site of consumption and use, most consumers are not aware of the conditions under which their products are made. As aptly stated by a toy industry executive, "the aura of fun and enchantment surrounding the global children's culture industry is only sustainable if conditions of production in the industry remain hidden from consumers" (Langer, 2004, p. 262). Thus, a cruel irony emerges: The company's marketing strategies imply that this product can "save girlhood"; meanwhile young Asian women face daily health hazards as they produce these dolls.

[23] As noted in chapter 2, compliance with GMP is 20% of a factory manager's performance evaluation, along with price, delivery, quality, and development of personnel, according to Professor S. Prakash Sethi, president of ICCA.

CHAPTER 5

The Käthe Kruse Doll Company

In this chapter I provide a brief history of the Käthe Kruse doll company and explore how it maintains tradition, ensures quality, and continually innovates to meet customer desires. This is not an easy balancing act, but a testament to its success is the fact that in 2005, the Käthe Kruse doll company celebrated its 100th anniversary. I also examine materials use, the work environment, and the control that workers have in the production process, as a way to consider these dolls in the context of the sustainable product design framework that I described in chapter 3.

In 1905, Käthe Kruse, a young German actress and artist, founded the company. She was married to the sculptor Max Kruse, who was 30 years her senior. When they began to have children, they moved to Montè Verita, an artistic, intellectual, and bohemian community near Ascona, Switzerland, where residents supported the values of pacifism, vegetarianism, and feminism (Murray, 2002). Max encouraged Käthe to make dolls for her children rather than purchase the heavy porcelain dolls sold in toy stores in German cities. Käthe used a potato for a head, a kitchen towel, sand, cotton and sawdust to make her first doll, which she gave to her 3-year-old daughter. Käthe continued to develop her doll designs and in 1910 was invited to exhibit her dolls. Following this successful exhibition, toy-shop owners began to ask her to make dolls for retail sale (Richter, 1984).

Reflecting the values she brought to doll making, Käthe Kruse developed a new doll design that greatly differed from most dolls produced commercially at the time. She believed that dolls should be primitive and natural, and that children should decide whether the doll was happy, sad, carefree, or frightened. She designed dolls that were meant to be played with and were soft, warm, and durable. Her dolls were stuffed with reindeer hair that warmed to the touch, giving them a lifelike quality. She aimed to produce a "child for the child" and cared greatly about the craft production of her "doll children." Said Kruse, "only the hand can create what proceeds from the hand to the heart" (Richter, 1984, p. 29). Like American women doll designers at the turn of the century, she created dolls that were safe, durable, and realistic, and that children could easily love (Formanek-Brunell, 1993).

In 1910 she contracted with the German company Kammer and Reinhardt to mass produce her doll designs but was very unhappy with the results and terminated the contract. She then set up her own doll-making workshop in Bad Kösen in eastern Germany. By the 1930s, Käthe Kruse was known in Germany as a master doll maker. An astute businesswoman, she also held true to her values of healthful living and careful artistry, including a caring and maternal attitude toward her 100 employees (Reinelt, 1994).

She faced a continual challenge: how to produce high-quality dolls that were also affordable. In 1950 her workshop in Bad Kösen in East Germany was taken over by the government and converted to a publicly owned entity.[1] The quality of the products declined as cheap materials were used, including plastic and celluloid for heads. Kruse was no longer involved in the design decisions. She then became a West German citizen and moved to the town of Donauwörth in Bavaria, where her sons Max and Michael had set up a doll-making operation in 1946. In 1952 her daughter Hanne and son-in-law Heinz Adler took control of the family business, gradually restoring it to its former level of quality. In 1956, Käthe Kruse fully turned the business over to her children (Lovaas, 1991).

In the late 1980s the Adlers looked for someone to take over the business who would carry on the principles and values of Käthe Kruse. In 1989 they found Andrea and Steve Christenson and sold the business to them for $2.8 million. The Christensons had previously worked at the Boston Consulting Group in Munich and were looking for a new business opportunity. As a child, Andrea had loved Käthe Kruse dolls, and as a businesswoman she greatly admired Käthe Kruse for her entrepreneurship over many decades. She was proud to become an owner of the company and determined to carry on the spirit of its founder. She and her husband divided up responsibilities for the company. As managing director, Steve was to focus on finance and production; as managing partner, Andrea would be responsible for product development and marketing.

THE KÄTHE KRUSE WORKSHOP

In October 2005 I visited the Käthe Kruse doll company, accompanied by a professional translator who lives in Berlin. We were cordially welcomed to the factory and were given a tour of the production process. Following this tour, we were given free access to the facility. We spent the next two and a half days on our own in the factory observing different aspects of the production process and informally interviewing employees. We scheduled formal interviews with the managing partner, production manager, purchasing agent, and doll "doctor." The quotations throughout this chapter are taken from those interviews.

---

[1] In the 1950s publicly owned enterprises or "Volkseigene Betriebe" (VEBs) incorporated 75% of East Germany's industrial sector (Curtis, 1992).

If you say Käthe Kruse, immediately people have an idea and impression. The brand is interlinked so strongly with the doll. Käthe Kruse with dolls is like Mercedes with cars. You know if it is a Käthe Kruse it is a safe and wonderful toy, nice and hand made . . . the doll is the synonym for Käthe Kruse. And the strength of the brand together with what you get is kind of intangible. Because it's a feeling of warmth. It's a feeling of the heart. It's a feeling of remembering. It's so many different aspects when you ask people: "I had a doll which was lost in the attic... I had a doll that I lost when I was fleeing the country". . . all these stories which people tell each other. And so I think this is the strength of the company. (Andrea Christenson)

The Käthe Kruse Workshop is located in Donauwörth, a quiet town of approximately 18,000, located at the confluence of the Danube and Wörnitz Rivers in the Bavarian region known as Swabia. Donauwörth is on a famous scenic route in Germany called the Romantic Road. It was a walled city; along the ancient Reichsstrasse, which runs through the town center, are buildings dating from 1297, 1499, and 1592. Many buildings were destroyed during World War II but most have since been restored. Traditional, conservative values remain strong in this region. Typical of Bavaria, 66% of Donauwörth residents are Catholic and 18% are Protestant.[2] In the 2005 election, more than 60% of Donauwörth voters cast ballots for the Christian Democratic Union (CDU), with 22% voting for the Social Democrats, 5% for the Green Party, and 6% for the Liberal Party.[3] Donauwörth has one of the lowest unemployment rates in Germany at 5.4%, little ethnic diversity and less of the racial tension that has surfaced in Berlin and other large German cities. Said Andrea Christenson, "Here, the world is still o.k."

Touring the Käthe Kruse Workshop in Donauwörth, one gets a feeling of stepping back in time. The workshop is a white stucco building set back from the main road with large windows and views of gardens. The workplace, bustling with activity, is very congenial. Dolls are everywhere: large soft cloth dolls sit on window sills in hallways, doll posters line the walls, finished dolls stand on display shelves, and boxes of dolls at various stages of the production process are visible throughout the workshop. The building is divided into many rooms where different aspects of production take place: doll and clothing design, stencil and fabric cutting, foam doll production, painting of doll faces, doll stuffing, head and wig attachment, doll dressing and hair styling, doll repair, and packing and shipping.

Rather than mass production on an assembly line, the company values craft production in a collegial atmosphere. In each room, several women sit near each other, intent on their own work, yet clearly enjoying the companionship of their fellow employees. Although our visit took place during the lead-up to the

[2]See www.donauwoerth.de
[3]http://www.bundestag.de/parliamet/wahlen/wahlen2005/wk255.html

Christmas season, a calmness pervaded the workplace. From all appearances, attention to detail and quality trumped any production quotas. Employees did not seemed rushed; once they got used to our presence they were comfortable taking the time to show us their role in the production process. They went out of their way to make sure we understood how the steps in the process fit together. For example, one of the doll stuffers arranged her work so that when we arrived on the second day she could demonstrate how she assembled the doll parts into a complete body. When we commented that we had not seen the stencil cutting of doll "skins," an employee took us into the stencil cutting room and showed us how she cut the doll body forms. When we noted that we had not observed the foam doll production, another employee brought us to the location of this activity and demonstrated how a foam doll form is made.

We were provided refreshments and lunch and all the interactions were polite and friendly. The most relaxed moment came when the doll designers, who had just celebrated one employee's birthday, offered us three different kinds of cake that they had made. The women laughed, chatted, shared recipes and asked us to join in rating their cakes. We could feel the close connection among these women and could imagine that it flowed into their creative work together. In each of the rooms we visited, we sensed comfort and camaraderie among the women working together; it seemed key to the stability of the workforce at the Käthe Kruse Workshop.

Andrea Christenson has worked hard to hold onto the traditions of the founder, Käthe Kruse. One is the use of high-quality natural materials. As Christenson told me, "for us it is important to work with natural materials that work with you." Yet she also acknowledges the need to compromise to meet functional requirements. For example, she wants to produce dolls and doll clothes that are easily washable. Therefore, soft dolls made for babies are stuffed with polypropylene pellets rather than wool. Handwork continues to be a central value, although some aspects of production are mechanized. Handwork includes sewing tiny details on the dolls and hand knitting and sewing clothes and accessories. The company avoids fads and has steered clear of creating fashion dolls or adding design features such as electronics.

> Sometimes a tradition is something wonderful . . . sometimes tradition can also limit. And to find the path. I will draw it. Like this is the mountain and then sometimes you have the young mountains like the Alps and they have peaks and crests. And the question is how you walk the crest with tradition and everything. And that's the challenge. (Andrea Christenson)

Innovation is a central aspect of Andrea Christenson's approach as well. She noted, "a sunflower is a nice flower . . . it follows the sun and goes to bed . . . to innovate you must [observe and] follow your environment—external and internal—to decide what to do next." In the last 15 years the Christensons have introduced several key product innovations. These include a line of Waldorf-style dolls that sell very well in the American market, play dolls made of vinyl and cloth that offer a more affordable option than the classic dolls produced primarily for adult collectors, and children's clothing and bedroom accessories. The company has been quite successful; annual sales were $18.8 million in 2005, up from $2.7 million when the Christensons purchased the company in 1989. It has also diversified its product offerings, with 40% of sales from dolls, 30% from baby and textile toys, 20% from children's clothing, and 10% from bedroom furnishings. Of the doll sales, Andrea Christenson estimates that 35% are purchased by adult collectors and 65% are purchased as children's toys. Käthe Kruse dolls are sold in specialty toy shops and high-end department stores, and in toy catalogues.

As the Christensons sought to expand into new production areas and needed additional labor, they considered a range of options and chose to purchase a factory in Latvia. This offered several advantages over outsourcing to Asian markets. Most important, they were able to build a trusting relationship with a local Latvian businessman who serves as production manager. They found in Latvia a readily available, well-educated female labor force. In addition, Latvia's proximity means that turn-around time is short and materials can be transported by truck between the two locations (driving takes 24 hours, air transport is 2 hours). By 2003, 90% of the company's production was occurring in Latvia. In 2006, the company employed approximately 700 people in Latvia and 85 in Donauwörth. Since Latvia joined the European Union in 2004 many people have left the country, seeking opportunities elsewhere in Europe. Wages have risen, but they are still considerably lower than in Germany, and home workers are available as well. As costs in Latvia increase, the company is exploring opportunities in neighboring Belarus.

Käthe Kruse's supply chain provides a picture of globalized production. The company has a range of suppliers, both nearby within Germany and the European Union and further afield in Asia. Supplier requirements differ depending on whether they are located in Europe or Asia. When asked whether they audit their European suppliers, Andrea Christenson replied that their European suppliers "are so high end that I would believe that their working conditions are also high end. None of them is a mass producer . . . the way they work is very special."

The Käthe Kruse doll company conducts laboratory tests in China and Germany to ensure that products meet EU safety standards and ASTM standards. They also receive certification by a third party, known as TÜV. The company requires its Asian suppliers to adhere to the Code of Business Practices developed by the International Council of Toy Industries.[4] The managing partner and production manager regularly visit the Chinese factory that produces the company's vinyl doll

---

[4]The International Council of Toy Industries Code of Business Practices is described in chapter 2.

parts so they have an opportunity to observe production processes and working conditions. However, because they inform the factory manager before they visit, the manager has time to prepare for their visits by cleaning up the factory.

The company uses some unusual materials, including reindeer hair from Scandinavia to stuff one type of classic doll, and human hair from India to produce wigs for all of the classic dolls. Employees at the Käthe Kruse workshop told us that Indian hair is preferable because of its strength. India, with an 85% Hindu population, has a seemingly limitless supply of human hair for wigs and other uses because of the Hindu practice of ritual tonsuring: shaving the head at least once in a lifetime. Temple priests bundle up the hair and sell it to Western sources, bringing India $20 million or more annually (Varadarajan, 2004). Large hair care companies such as L'Oreal process the hair, by cleaning, dyeing and/or bleaching, and then styling it. They then sell it to enterprises such as Käthe Kruse for the blonde wigs of the classic German dolls.

Textiles, including cotton and wool, are a significant material input into the production process of Käthe Kruse products as they are used for doll "skins," doll clothes and children's clothes. The company purchases textiles from Switzerland, Austria, Spain, Germany, and France. According to Käthe Kruse employees, 99% of the textiles purchased as input materials for the dolls are certified to the Öko-Tex Standard 100, which is designed to protect the consumer from harmful chemicals.[5] Approximately 20% of the cotton fabric purchased is organic; however, the company is now launching a new line of 100% organic fabric.[6]

THE DESIGN PROCESS

You are always thinking of something new. . . . This is a constant thing in your head. So, whatever you are looking at, you are questioning, is this right or should we do it differently? You have to be careful not to do it too often because then you have chaos. But it should not be too long because then a product will be either boring or outdated. So you have to find the right timing. It is about timing and it is about understanding the user's need, i.e., consumer need. Everybody is a consumer. (Andrea Christenson)

The Käthe Kruse doll company employs designers to focus on different aspects of the operation: clothing for the classic and play dolls, Waldorf doll design, soft toy design, and play doll design. The design room is full of activity and energy: the women who design the prototypes, make the patterns, and then

---

[5] The Öko-tex 100 standard is described in chapter 2.

[6] According to the Pesticides Action Network, cotton production uses approximately 10% of the the world's pesticides and almost 25% of the world's insecticides, creating hazards for workers and the environment (see www.panna.org). Companies such as Käthe Kruse support the growth of organic cotton by specifying this requirement.

sew the prototypes work alongside each other and share ideas in a rapid-fire exchange. The sewer said, "When there's a feeling of harmony in the room then it really boosts the creativity also. The way it is right now it's really very good . . . you can notice what [comes out of it]."

The doll clothing designer works closely with Andrea Christenson to select fabrics for the doll clothing. Many of the design concepts flow from the fabrics themselves and then are influenced by the group dynamic. As the designer noted, "It's always as a team . . . I might draw a sketch and then someone else says, oh, maybe it would be good this way or that way and when you go to do it, the pattern, it changes."

Andrea Christenson gives final approval to the designs before the prototypes are created. Cost is not a major consideration with the classic dolls, which are made in small quantities, primarily for adult collectors. Special materials such as cashmere are used and details are included such as hand sewing and knitting. With the play dolls, cost is a consideration as the designers choose fabrics and other materials. But the designer of play doll clothes has more creative freedom in choosing fabrics. The designer of doll clothing told us, "there's a little bit less special work . . . for the play dolls I can really use colors and all kinds of things. It can be a little crazy."

One of the doll designers works only on making Waldorf-style dolls. She explained that color is what matters most to her as her doll designs flow from the colors of the fabrics: "Sometimes I'll just look at the different fabrics and get ideas for what to do with it. But the color is what's really attractive. I wanted to make rainbow dolls for years, but never found fabric in all the rainbow colors. And then it worked all of a sudden."

Another designer creates toys that are soft and cuddly, using natural materials. She is guided by the philosophy of Käthe Kruse. When asked if this approach limits her as a designer, she replied: "that is my philosophy and why I came to work at Käthe Kruse . . . as a four-year-old I got my first Käthe Kruse doll. And it never quite let me go."

THE PRODUCTION PROCESS

The Käthe Kruse doll company manufactures five different types of dolls. These include three types of classic dolls: dolls stuffed with reindeer hair, and soft and hard polyurethane foam dolls. Two types of play dolls have been introduced in the last decade: one made of vinyl or a combination of vinyl/foam and vinyl/cloth, and Waldorf dolls made of natural materials. Approximately 15,000 classic dolls, 25,000 play dolls, and 50,000 Waldorf dolls are produced each year.

The production method for classic dolls has changed little over the past century, and remains both hands-on and labor intensive, despite some innovations in materials and production processes. Each classic doll takes approximately 20 hours to complete, and passes through the hands of eight to ten craftspeople.

The reindeer-hair dolls are stuffed by hand in a process that takes six to eight hours. Workers use wooden dowels to firmly tamp down the reindeer hair, creating a fine dust as they work. The bodies of the polyurethane foam dolls are produced in the Donauwörth workshop and then covered with a "skin" of cotton stockinet. These skins are cut out by using a stencil machine and then are sewn by home workers. A local factory produces the polystyrene heads for these dolls. The doll faces are painted before they are attached by hand to the doll body. The face painting begins with machine-spraying a stencil design and then details and shading are added by hand, requiring up to eight steps. As one painter noted, "the foundation [spraying on the stencil] is a technical piece of work. In the 21st century it would be an anachronism to do that by hand. It's what comes on top of the foundation that is the art and gives the doll its character."

Once the doll parts are stuffed and the arms, legs and head are attached to the body, the workers glue on the wigs and style the doll hair. The dolls are then dressed and made ready for packaging and shipping. All the classic dolls have human hair wigs, which are hand-knotted by home workers. These wigs take an experienced worker approximately six hours to complete. Employees iron and starch doll clothes that have been made in Latvia and dress each doll. Finally, the hairdresser styles each doll's hair as required for a particular design: she may cut, braid, and/or curl the hair and may attach ribbons.

Packaging is done in an adjacent room. Dolls are placed in printed cardboard boxes that indicate they meet European and U.S. toy safety standards. Packing materials include bubble wrap, foam, and air-filled plastic packaging. Different types of packing materials are used as needed to protect the items inside. The dolls are shipped by truck or rail within Europe and by air to more distant destinations. It did not appear that the company pays special attention to using environmentally sound packaging materials or processes. However, the packers reuse packing materials and boxes as a matter of course.

Beginning in the late 1990s, the company introduced play dolls made of PVC in combinations of vinyl/cloth and vinyl/foam. The PVC is specified to be free of phthalates and heavy metals. When asked if she had questions about using PVC as a production material, Andrea Christenson replied, "I don't have questions about it, because it seems to be a material that the mothers as well as the children like. And there are certain things that are easier to make in the vinyl than in the [polystyrene]." Each mold for the vinyl dolls costs approximately $1000 to $2000, depending on its size, while each mold for the polystyrene heads (for the classic dolls) costs approximately $25,000. The lower production costs make the vinyl dolls much more affordable than the classic dolls. In addition, the vinyl material is more durable than the polystyrene. Some vinyl dolls are weighted with quartz sand and others with polyethylene pellets. The vinyl doll parts are produced in China and arrive at the Donauwörth and Latvian factories with synthetic hair called kanekalon. In Donauwörth and Latvia, the dolls' faces are painted, their hair is styled, and they are dressed and packaged.

In the late 1990s the company introduced Waldorf dolls, which have been very successful, particularly in the American market. The German Waldorf Organization in Stuttgart, Germany, has certified the dolls, so the company can label them with a "W" in its catalog, indicating that the doll is made of natural materials such as wool, cotton, mohair, and linen. The intention behind this marketing approach is to attract the Waldorf school market in Germany and the United States. Another benefit of this certification is that these toys can be marketed as "eco-friendly" to attract an additional group of consumers.

Once the Waldorf doll prototypes are approved, these dolls are produced at the Latvian facility. They are stuffed with wool and covered with a cotton stocking. Each Waldorf doll is unique because of the head design, which begins as a ball of wool. Thread is wrapped around the ball in two directions creating a distinctive head shape. A tiny ball of wool is used for the nose. The head is then covered with a cotton stocking and the body is stuffed with wool as well. The eyes and mouth are drawn or sewn on with yarn and soft natural materials are used to make clothing and hair. Because this entire process is done by hand, no two dolls are exactly alike. The company also makes Waldorf-style dolls that do not have the "W" label. As described earlier, some compromises are necessary to meet functionality requirements, such as filling the Waldorf-style baby toys with poly-ethylene pellets rather than wool to ensure that they can be washed easily.

Another important aspect of the production process is doll repair. The company employs a "Puppendoktor" (doll doctor) to catalog and oversee the repair of over 3000 dolls each year; they are sent to Donauwörth from all over the world. Many of these are old dolls that have been discovered in attics or tucked away in trunks; others are the newer play dolls and Waldorf dolls. The doll doctor estimates the costs of repair, which may involve attaching new limbs, restuffing, painting, reattaching a wig, or styling hair. Customers are charged for the cost of the repairs and shipping. The doll doctor told us, "you're not only writing . . . the estimates . . . sometimes you have to talk to the customer . . . you have to explain the [repairs needed]. They write it down and you hear many stories about the doll . . . it's quite an interesting job."

HEALTH AND SAFETY ISSUES IN PRODUCTION

One of the major occupational hazards of the textile/apparel industry is the repetitive motion required to use a sewing machine, which may result in repetitive strain injuries. This did not appear to be a major concern at the Käthe Kruse workshop in Donauwörth.[7] Although machine sewing is a major component of

---

[7]Although I did not have the opportunity to observe home workers or workers at the Latvian facility (where 90% of production occurs), I was informed that the production process there is similar to what I observed in Donauwörth.

Stuffing reindeer hair into a doll body.

Foam doll bodies.

Stencil cutting doll skins.

Painting a doll's face.

Doll hairdressing.

Dolls ready to be dressed.

Dressing the dolls.

Dolls waiting for repair.

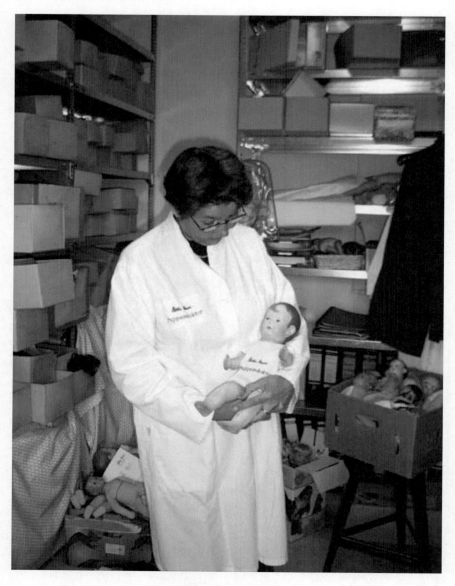

The "Puppendoktor."

Friedebald and Ilsebill—classic dolls.

Lolle—vinyl play doll.

Mini It's me—Waldorf cloth dolls.

production at the company, workers also do a significant amount of handwork and are not tied to an assembly line. When I asked them about health, safety, and ergonomic concerns, workers indicated that they were tired at the end of the day but "you get used to it." The process of stuffing a doll skin with reindeer hair takes a significant amount of force and may result in sore arm muscles. One way that workers address these concerns is by rotating among their different job responsibilities so that they do not spend an entire workday repeating the same motions. By shifting to another aspect of their job, they can reduce the strain on a particular body part or set of muscles.

Although workers at Käthe Kruse experience high demands at certain times in the production cycle, they have a fair amount of autonomy in determining how they get their jobs done, which may moderate stress and muscle strain. This follows the prediction of the "demand-control" model that was introduced in chapter 3. According to this model, jobs that combine high demand with low control over the work process are particularly risky, whereas jobs with high demand and high control are less risky (Karasek, 1992).

The company provides semi-annual training about the safe use of chemicals and machinery.[8] The production of polyurethane foam involves the use of two industrial chemicals, methylene diphenyl diisocyanate (MDI) and polyol, which present a hazard for workers, and for the community in the event of an accidental release. MDI can irritate the skin, eyes, and respiratory tract. Chronic exposure to MDI can sensitize the skin or respiratory tract, which may lead to asthma. In the early 1990s, the company stopped using toluene diisocyanate, classified by the International Agency for Research on Cancer as possibly carcinogenic to humans (National Institute for Occupational Safety and Health [NIOSH], 2004). The production of polystyrene doll heads may pose additional occupational hazards, as styrene is a mutagen and neurotoxin. This process occurs off-site at a factory that makes these doll heads for the Käthe Kruse doll company.

The cutting machines have very sharp blades and pose an additional occupational hazard. The production manager noted that a cut finger was the only accident that had occurred during his 15 years working at the factory.

An additional occupational health issue is the use of solvents in the painting room. The paints themselves are of low toxicity, and since the 1990s, most glues and cleaning agents used in the production process have been water-based. However, a solvent odor emanated from the painting room, as petroleum-based solvents are used for cleaning paint brushes. Chronic exposure to petroleum-based solvents can damage the central nervous system. In a second room where the paint-spraying operation is conducted, there is a hood and exhaust ventilation system, which is checked annually to ensure that it is operating properly.

WORKPLACE FLEXIBILITY AND WORKER CONTROL OVER JOB TASKS

Käthe Kruse inspired loyalty in her workers by insuring that her production schedules could accommodate workers' family lives and Andrea Christenson has carried on this philosophy. The Donauwörth workshop employs approximately 85 people, and the factory in Latvia employs about 700. In both locations, approximately 95% of employees are female. Many employees have a part-time schedule and hours are flexible. Andrea Christenson notes:

> for our system to work . . . our hours [have to] work around the women's schedules . . . some ladies come at 6 A.M. and in summer sometimes at 5 A.M. and work and go home by 2 P.M. And we have a lot of part-time people. Or people that work at night, they start at 4 P.M. and they go home at 9 P.M. . . . we can do that. Because we are not a typical production place.

[8]The company is not unionized, although under German law, workers could choose to form a union or to join the textile union.

Of the 12 employees I interviewed, all but one (a very recent hire) had worked at the company for over 10 years; several had been employed over 20 years. Some of the women noted that they had left employment at Käthe Kruse to have children and had returned later, often in positions of greater responsibility. During one informal conversation a worker remarked that she would not become a millionaire but she liked her job. Wages are average for the textile industry, but lower than in the electronics sector. In 2005, the average wage at the Donauwörth facility was $12.70/hour; for home workers the average wage was $10/hour. In 2005, at the factory in Latvia the average wage for factory and home workers was $2.20/hour.

Historically, the company has hired many home workers. New regulations, however, have raised the wages for home workers, making this option less profitable for the company, and decreasing the cost differential between home and factory workers. Now the Donauwörth workshop employs only 10 to 15 home workers. These workers machine-stitch the muslin and stockinet skins for the classic dolls, hand-knot the human hair wigs, sew doll clothes, and make Waldorf dolls. In Latvia the company employs approximately 50 home workers. In fact, home and factory may be more connected than one would expect. Workers at Donauwörth told me that in Latvia the children of employees often come to the factory after school and do their homework there. This arrangement serves as informal childcare, and, according to interviewees, did not entail any child labor.

Workers appreciate the fact that they are not pressed to meet daily production quotas and that they are not tied to an assembly line doing one repetitive task after another. One doll maker told us, "I like to put the whole doll together, just because it's some variety. It's not so monotonous." A general rule of the production process at the company is that each craftsperson is responsible for a doll as a whole. For example, a doll stuffer will also attach the arms, legs, and head, so that she fully constructs that doll before it is taken to be dressed and have its hair styled. This approach ensures quality, as the worker will evaluate the doll as a whole to make sure it stands and the body parts are balanced; it also may increase worker satisfaction, as employees are responsible for creating a whole object, rather than being a "cog in a wheel" as in a typical assembly line.

In addition, most workers are cross-trained so that they can take on different aspects of production as needed. The production manager explained, "We are a very small company so that if everyone has one specific job then they can only do that job and if one person is sick then everything stops. So they all had to learn other jobs . . . everyone has three or four different jobs that they can do . . . it is not like they forget how to do one of them. So if at any time someone is sick, someone else can jump in—and so we can have a lot more flexibility." For example, if an order comes in for 100 dolls of a certain type, a hairdresser or wig attacher can assist with dressing the dolls to prepare them for packing. This cross-training benefits the production process as workers can be directed to areas requiring additional support, and it also may benefit workers psychologically and ergonomically as they engage in a variety of work tasks throughout the day.

It is interesting to step back and review the path this company has taken over 100 years. Käthe Kruse's act of genius in 1905 was to design a doll that provided a soft, gentle, realistic, informal, and safe alternative to the heavy, fancy, formal porcelain dolls common at the turn of the century. She designed a high-quality doll that was durable and could be repaired. For over a century the brand has been well known for these qualities. The Christensons have carried on this tradition of quality and at the same time have introduced innovations to keep their company profitable. By emphasizing craft production, the company has maintained the quality of its product and sustained a work environment that is satisfying for workers because of the varied skills required in the production process and the flexibility of workplace policies that accommodate workers' needs.

In 2008 the classic Käthe Kruse dolls seem somewhat anachronistic as a child's plaything, at least from a U.S. perspective. Though exquisite, they are stiff, formal, and old-fashioned, and hardly the radical alternative they represented in 1905. They are now created primarily for adults who are serious doll collectors. In contrast, the cloth and vinyl play dolls introduced by Käthe Kruse's new owners in the last decade are up-to-date and very appealing to children.

The company has successfully expanded into new product areas including Waldorf dolls and toys and vinyl dolls. These successful new product types represent a divergence of values, choices, and directions for the company. The choice to develop Waldorf toys and dolls means choosing natural materials— continuing the company's appreciation of handmade objects—and marketing the products as natural and eco-friendly. The choice to create vinyl and vinyl/cloth play dolls represents a move toward mass production and a greater emphasis on synthetic materials. These two survival strategies in the toy world may seem to be in conflict, but they also illustrate the need for multiple approaches in a competitive industry and compromises that allow a company to remain profitable.

CHAPTER 6

The Q'ewar Project of Andahuaylillas, Peru

The Q'ewar House (pronounced Kaywar), set high above the village of Andahuaylillas in Peru, looks out at the velvety green mountains of the Andes. In the early morning the mountains are often shrouded in a silvery gray mist, but by mid-morning the Andean sun shines through and the sky is a brilliant blue. The setting is tranquil, far from the town square or the activity of the local market.

The young women of the Q'ewar Project arrive at 8 A.M. with their children in tow. After bringing the children to the on-site nursery the workers begin the day by cleaning their workshops. The project has four rooms for different aspects of production: a "large doll" workshop, a "medium/small doll" workshop, a workshop for knitting and preparing alpaca yarn, and a workshop for cutting and sewing doll skins and doll clothing. Each workshop is designed for three to four women to work together. The adobe workspaces are clean, airy, and light-filled with large windows and views of the mountains, cornfields, and flower gardens. The design of the work environment is intentionally calm and peaceful. No radio blares and no posters hang on the whitewashed walls. The Q'ewar women are encouraged to converse and create community with one another as they work, as an important element of this enterprise is empowering each of these young women to find her own voice.

The women settle in for several hours of doll making, picking up from wherever they stopped the evening before. At 10 A.M., a woman calls "maté, senoras" and all the workers assemble on the stone patio for herbal tea and a snack of dried roasted corn. After this 15-minute social break the women resume their work until noon, when they pick up their children from the nursery and head home for lunch and rest time until 2 P.M. At 2 P.M. the doll-making work resumes, punctuated by an afternoon maté break at 4 P.M., and then work concludes at 6 P.M. Most women work full-time Monday through Friday and also come to work on alternate Saturdays for knitting workshops and to help when women come from the rural villages to spin alpaca fiber. If a Q'ewar worker cannot work because of family obligations, she simply informs the project directors. Workers are paid by the day, and their salary is adjusted for any days or half days of work that they miss.

Julio Herrera Burgos and Lucy Terrazas, the founders and directors of the Q'ewar Project, view themselves as equals with the doll makers and have designed a primarily horizontal organization. No one is given orders; rather, the workers are asked politely to participate in the daily activities of the doll-making project. Equality, mutual respect, and responsibility to one's work are the most important values Julio and Lucy espouse as project directors.

I visited the Q'ewar Project for a week in March 2006. Knowing that the project founders and workers spoke Spanish and Quechua (one of the indigenous languages of the Andes), I invited an interpreter who was fluent in Spanish to accompany me. The project directors generously offered us room and board at the Q'ewar House. We had unlimited access to all aspects of the doll-making operation. We spent much of the week observing workers in various aspects of the production process. I conducted four in-depth interviews with the project founders (three with Julio and one with Lucy) to learn about the design process and to understand the program philosophy and approach. The quotations throughout this chapter are taken from those interviews.

According to Julio, the Q'ewar doll is unique because of the community and harmony in which it is made. He views the Q'ewar doll making as "social art," which he describes as art designed to awaken the creative capacity in human beings, without inflating their egos. The intent of the Q'ewar Project is to build a shared cultural and social community that benefits everyone. Paraphrasing the artist Paul Klee, Julio said, "art does not reproduce what is visible; rather it makes visible [what is spiritual]." Julio believes that a person's spiritual aspects can be tapped as they engage in handwork in community with others. In this way, the doll maker becomes an intermediary, transmitting a spiritual intention to the product being made.

The importance of a tranquil work environment cannot be overstated. The Q'ewar Project founders believe that unhappy workers cannot create a doll that will be healthy for a child. As Lucy told me, "anxious, desperate, or sick women cannot make these dolls." Julio and Lucy believe that a calm and healthy workplace, in combination with artistic handwork, can provide a healing and therapeutic environment for these workers who have experienced extreme hardship. According to Julio, human dignity is the most important consideration, above and beyond the product itself. When attention is paid to the human dignity of the worker, she can make a product that is healthy for a child.

Julio and Lucy view this initiative very broadly as a social development effort that can eventually benefit the entire community of Andahuaylillas. The production of dolls is a way to provide a sustainable livelihood, but it is only one aspect of a wider effort to provide education, medical care, economic self-sufficiency, and ultimately empowerment to the Q'ewar workers.[1] How did this remarkable enterprise come about?

THE INITIATION OF THE Q'EWAR PROJECT

Julio Herrera Burgos, age 54, a Peruvian sculptor and educator, is the visionary behind the Q'ewar Project. Julio was trained in economics, education, and art (drawing, painting, and sculpture) and has wide-ranging experience as a teacher and artist. He taught art at a Waldorf high school in Lima, Peru, and later came to Cusco, Peru, to teach sculpture at a fine arts school for adults. Julio sees the Q'ewar Project as a manifestation of his continually evolving spiritual path. He has been greatly influenced by the writings of Rudolf Steiner, a German philosopher and teacher known for his educational theories, which came to be known as Waldorf education. Steiner connected the "three ideals of universal humanity—liberty, equality, and fraternity" with the cultural, political, and social development of humans and with the education of children (Childs, 1991, pp. 4-5). Julio's long-term vision for the Q'ewar Project is of a fully integrated human community that acts together to support social, economic, political, and cultural development for everyone.

In 2000 Julio and his life partner Lucy Terrazas, age 52, decided to live in Andahuaylillas, a small community of 5200 people located about an hour by bus from the city of Cusco. In 2002 Julio brought his Cusco art students to the village to create large stone sculptures, which are displayed in the main plaza today.

As Julio and Lucy settled into the community, they became aware that local residents greatly needed meaningful work to sustain and empower them economically, especially the young women. Traditional Andean communities are strongly gendered, with males and females seen as having complementary roles (Heckman, 2003). Women care for children, pasture livestock (such as cows, alpaca, and sheep), help tend agricultural fields, and manage family resources. Men are generally in charge of farming and construction and often are the primary wage earners for their families.

After befriending Julio and Lucy, several women asked them for work. Many women in Andahuaylillas begin having children in their teens. These young women are often unmarried and have no economic assistance from a male partner. Although it is difficult to determine the prevalence of domestic violence in any community, it appears to be common in the villages of the Peruvian Andes and is almost always connected to alcohol abuse (Estremadoyro, 2001). Young women in these Peruvian communities tend to have little authority or decision-making power and have access to few resources, which may make them particularly vulnerable to domestic violence (Ross, 2001).

---

[1] In chapter 1, I introduced the term "sustainable livelihoods" (Braidotti et al., 1994, p. 90).

For many years, Julio had thought about making Waldorf dolls. As a teacher in Lima and Buenos Aires, he had taught students to make marionettes. In the 1990s, Julio traveled to Germany and Switzerland and learned more about marionette making and Waldorf doll design. He saw that Waldorf dolls sold well in Germany and met someone who expressed interest in purchasing dolls. When the young women of Andahuaylillas described their need for work, Julio saw that he could realize his dream of making dolls. He believed that this work could provide a sustainable livelihood and could also be spiritually nourishing to these women whose lives were very difficult. Using a supply of wool that he had purchased to make mattresses, he and Lucy launched the Q'ewar Project.

What began in 2002 as a very small project in the home of Julio and Lucy has now expanded to support twenty-six full-time female doll makers and six men who work in construction and agriculture on the Q'ewar House property. In addition, the project supports approximately 35 women from rural villages who come to the Q'ewar House to spin alpaca fiber twice a month and a rural family that weaves doll ponchos and shawls. Because one goal is to create sustainable livelihoods for as many people as possible, the project employs women to spin, card, and clean alpaca fiber. Julio explained that although they could easily eliminate the jobs of the women doing the spinning and carding by purchasing industrially prepared fiber, doing so would be contrary to his vision for this initiative.

As the project grew, Julio and Lucy purchased a piece of land on the hillside above the main part of town. Julio arranged for the construction of an adobe dwelling that now includes living space for Julio and Lucy, two small guest rooms for visitors and volunteers, four workshop spaces, and a nursery for the workers' children. Outside the dwelling are patio spaces for the many women who come on the weekends to spin alpaca fiber, along with bathrooms for the Q'ewar workers, a large organic garden, and corn and potato fields. The male Q'ewar workers are currently building a structure that will be used for a sculpture workshop and can house volunteers; a schoolhouse is also under construction.

Julio is the artistic visionary for the project and is closely involved in the doll design and production process. He is also the buyer of all the materials, so he must travel frequently throughout the region. In addition, Julio communicates with doll distributors in the United States and Europe. Lucy serves as the day-to-day production manager. She oversees the work of the women in each workshop and notifies Julio when supplies are running low. She also supervises the design and production of doll clothing. In addition, she is in charge of stocking the Q'ewar retail shop with dolls and other items. Lucy also administers the nursery and trains the childcare workers to ensure that the children are well treated, have nutritious food, and are taught basic hygiene. Because Lucy is fluent in Quechua, she plays a key communication role on Saturdays when the Quechua-speaking women come from the rural villages.

In addition to her work with the Q'ewar project Lucy is an elected member of the mayor's staff for the community of Andahuaylillas. This gives her the opportunity to be involved in supporting community development projects throughout the region and to meet others who are engaged in these efforts.

Both Julio and Lucy model the basic values of the Q'ewar Project—respect for others and responsibility to one's work—and address any incidents that are at odds with these values. For example, during the week I visited, a conflict arose in one of the workshops. Julio asked the women to put down their work and talk with each other to resolve the conflict. Over the past few years, several women who did not show respect to others or were not responsible in their work have been asked to leave the project; however, this has been a rare occurrence.

Most of the women of the Q'ewar Project are in their early 20s and have one or more children. About half have completed secondary school and half have completed a few years of primary school. Some of the women joined the project when it was initiated four years ago; others have joined more recently. Each woman came to the Q'ewar Project with no knowledge of doll making and was trained by Julio and Lucy, not only in the technical aspects of the production process but also in the philosophy of the workplace.

The atmosphere of the workplace, with its intention of community building, is a very different environment from what most of these women have experienced in their lives so far. Therefore, for many of them, meeting Julio's and Lucy's expectations for daily behavior did not come naturally at first; it required practice and discussion as a group. At first, these women were extremely quiet in their workshops, but they slowly became more comfortable conversing, even with Julio and Lucy around. Now Julio and Lucy know each of these women well, including the details of their often difficult lives. Many of the Q'ewar workers now refer to Julio and Lucy as "Papa Julio" and "Mama Lucy." These terms of endearment reflect the close relationships that have developed as the participants experience the values of the Q'ewar Project on a daily basis.

THE DESIGN PROCESS

There are four types of Q'ewar dolls: the original Q'ewar doll (16 inches), the bambino (also 16 inches with a larger head and dressed in baby clothes), the medium doll (9 inches), and the small doll (6 inches). The basic form of the Q'ewar doll comes from Waldorf education principles: the doll should be soft and made of natural materials, and it should stimulate the imagination of young children (up to age 7). The doll has eyes and a mouth but no nose. This design is purposeful, as Rudolf Steiner's philosophy of human spirituality suggests that leaving something unfinished activates a child's imagination. Because a young child sees the whole and does not focus on the details, these details are unnecessary (Steiner, 1996). In addition, the doll is designed so that it does not give a sexual message, as it should not awaken premature sexuality in children. Julio noted that these dolls can be seen as "anti-Barbie" in that they have no breasts or short skirts.

The doll design process is iterative and takes consumer feedback into account. Julio knows each of the doll vendors and encourages them to solicit comments from their customers. For example, when the dolls were first sold, customers complained that the arms were too stiff, so the arms were adjusted. The doll prototypes are also tested in the Q'ewar nursery. One prototype had a nose formed in the face, but as the children played with the doll the cloth wore through at the nose. Since, as noted above, an unfinished face may stimulate a child's imagination, the project directors decided to eliminate the nose from the design. The medium dolls were introduced to attract consumers who already own a large-sized Waldorf doll and want a smaller version to add to their collection. The smallest dolls were designed as an accessory to fit on the backs of the large dolls, to be carried in a shawl called a manta. These medium and small dolls are less expensive and have proven to be very popular.

The Q'ewar dolls differ from many other Waldorf-style dolls in that the arms and legs are stuffed separately from the head and torso and then sewed on so that they can rotate 360 degrees. The arms and legs are properly aligned with the body and the outlines of the hands and feet are apparent, making the dolls appear very lifelike, even with unfinished faces. This differs from some Waldorf designs that have balls for hands and feet. The doll clothing is designed so that young children can easily take the clothes off and put them back on. Color is an important element in the clothing design process. To meet a range of customer tastes, some of the Q'ewar doll clothing is designed to display vivid contrasts using complementary colors and some is designed with softer, pastel colors. Another aspect of doll clothing design is the use of local materials such as alpaca thread, sheep's wool, and bayeta, a coarsely woven cloth made of sheep's wool.

The design of doll clothing is also an iterative process. Lucy oversees clothing design with the two expert designers/seamstresses. Originally all the dolls were clothed in indigenous dress and had the dark hair of the indigenous people of Peru. However, European and North American buyers have asked for dolls with blond and red hair wearing European and North American styles of clothing rather than indigenous dress. The Q'ewar Project has begun producing these dolls, preserving some uniquely Peruvian elements by using materials such as bayeta and alpaca. New clothing designs are introduced approximately every 6 months.

THE PRODUCTION PROCESS

The doll-making process begins with the processing of alpaca fiber. Then workers cut and dye doll skins, stuff the dolls, add hair and limbs, and finally add the eyes and mouth and dress the dolls. The alpaca wool is used for the doll hair and clothing. On alternate Saturdays approximately 35 women from rural villages come to the Q'ewar House to spin the alpaca fiber using drop spindles, a traditional activity of many Peruvian women of the Andes. They arrive in groups of two or three, with babies tied to their backs in brightly woven cloths. Each woman finds a spot on the stone patio that surrounds the adobe house and they spend the day chatting and spinning. If the day is rainy, they can work in a covered shelter that is also used as a carpentry workshop. The women first sort the alpaca fiber by color and then use various techniques for hand spinning. Some wind the fiber around their arms and others put the drop spindle between their toes to facilitate the spinning process. This work appears almost effortless, as these women have been spinning alpaca fiber with such seamless motions since they were young girls. When they have completely spun the fiber, they roll it into a ball.

The next step is cleaning the newly spun alpaca yarn. Workers unwind the yarn into loose lengths, which they then wash and dry. Much of the alpaca yarn is used in its natural color, which may be white, or various shades of brown or black. Some of the white alpaca yarn is dyed on-site in a large metal pot.

The Q'ewar Project is experimenting with traditional dyeing processes that utilize plants and insects, such as cochineal, a red dye derived from a beetle that feeds on cactus plants. The workers crush dried beetle exoskeletons using a mortar and pestle, creating a vivid color that ranges from pink to purple to red. They collect the colored powder and add lime juice if a redder color is desired. Over a wood fire, they boil water with alum, a fixative. The next day they place the cochineal powder in cloth sacks and boil them in the water solution for an hour. They then add yarn and boil it for 45 minutes. They then rinse the yarn and dry it in the shade to avoid fading from the sun. Effluent from the process goes directly onto the ground or down the sink into a septic system.[2]

The first step in producing the doll bodies is cutting, sewing, and dyeing the doll "skins." The cutters use cardboard patterns to draw the needed shapes on the cotton fabric. They cut out the skins by hand and sew them together using a foot treadle sewing machine. The cotton purchased for the skins has an orange tint, so they dye the skins in strong black tea to make the skin color more natural. They soak the skins thoroughly in water and then wring them out. They pour the tea over the fabric, add salt and hot water, and boil the mixture for a half hour. Then they rinse the fabric and hang it indoors to dry.

The next stage is stuffing. The large dolls are stuffed with sheep's wool that is purchased already carded and cleaned. Originally the Q'ewar workers did the

---

[2]Much of Peru lacks adequate wastewater treatment. The Q'ewar House's on-site septic drainage system was already one quarter full in March 2006. Liquid wastes and gray water from cooking, laundry, and bathing become part of the irrigation system. When I visited, the nearest sewage treatment plant was not operating because of maintenance problems. Many rivers are polluted as sewage and solid waste go directly into them without treatment.

carding and cleaning of sheep's wool, but this work was found to be very labor intensive. The medium and small dolls are stuffed with sheep's wool or with alpaca if fiber is left over that is not suitable for spinning. The worker uses a plastic tube to help move the stuffing deep into the arm or leg part. One challenge is to make the dolls firm, but not too firm, as customers have commented that the dolls were too stiff.

Once she has stuffed the arms and legs, the worker then creates the doll's head. This head is a classic Waldorf form. The skin is stuffed with wool, and then two strings are tied around the head, one vertical and one horizontal. The horizontal string is pulled partway down, giving the head its characteristic shape. Then the head is covered with a cotton skin that will hold the head form and the doll torso. When the torso is fully stuffed, it is sewn shut. Next, the head is carefully sewn to the body to create an indentation that forms a neck shape.

The next step is the most time-consuming in the entire doll-making process: sewing on the hair. There are six different hairstyle types: for female dolls, three types of braids, and for male dolls, curly hair, straight hair with bangs, or straight hair parted on the side. The curly style is the most labor-intensive, taking a worker approximately one full day to sew on a large doll; the other hairstyles take a half day to complete. Alpaca yarn is used for the doll hair. Most of the alpaca yarn for hair is spun on-site, but industrially produced alpaca yarn is also purchased when supplies run low. Julio draws an outline on each head to indicate the hairstyle and hair placement and the Q'ewar workers use this frame to stitch the hair in place.

When the doll hair is completely sewn, the workers attach the arms and legs. Now the doll is beginning to look human. At this stage in the production process Julio and Lucy become directly engaged. Julio sews the eyes and mouth of each doll. Lucy is responsible for the final step of production. She dresses each doll, choosing either complementary colors that will provide a strong contrast or pastel colors for a softer look. From start to finish, it takes approximately 40 hours to complete a large doll, 15 hours to complete a medium doll, and 8 hours to complete a small doll.

The Q'ewar workers are taught to control for quality throughout the production process by using tape measures to check sizing and by feeling each doll to ensure it is not too stiff. Julio and Lucy are involved at the final stages of production to provide another check for product quality and also to ensure that the dolls are attired as the vendors requested.

Doll clothing is created concurrently with the production of doll bodies. Leading this aspect of the operation, in consultation with Lucy, are two women who have taught themselves to design and sew clothing. One woman is responsible for producing the clothing for all the large-sized dolls. She works from her home and involves her two grown sons, and her husband and 10-year-old daughter in the production process. She is very skilled at creating "typical dress" for the dolls, that is, clothing that is indigenous to particular villages in the

Cusco region of Peru. She grew up in a village in this region and after learning to sew began making costumes for young dancers traveling to Europe to perform traditional Andean dancing. She and her family produce 600 to 700 pieces of clothing per month, and are paid by the piece. She works mostly from memory, without patterns. Some of the Q'ewar women help with the sewing of the large doll clothes, for example, by sewing undergarments.

Another talented seamstress is responsible for designing and producing clothing for the medium-sized dolls. Also self-taught, she is very interested in finding styles that will appeal to North American and European consumers. She is also an expert knitter and teaches knitting to the Q'ewar workers. The dolls are attired in many knitted items, including sweaters, hats, and booties. Some of the knitting takes place at the Q'ewar House. One of the Q'ewar workers has learned to use a hand-operated knitting machine, which speeds up the process of making the doll sweaters, though handwork is still required to complete the sweater. Much of the knitting, however, occurs off-site. The rural women who come to Q'ewar on Saturday bring sweaters, booties, and hats that they have knitted and they are paid for each piece.

Several rural villagers weave doll ponchos for the male dolls and shawls known as mantas for the female dolls. The most prolific weaver is a 20-year-old who works with his family members to produce brightly colored lengths of fabric, which can then be cut to the right size. This family uses chemical dyes containing aniline, without any fixative, so the Q'ewar workers have to wash the fabric to remove excess dye.[3] This produces wastewater containing chemical residues, which goes directly into the ground untreated.

Since the initiative began, Julio and Lucy have had a vision that they would eventually provide this family with plant-dyed yarns for weaving, so that they could stop using aniline dyes. In April 2006, to teach the workers some plant-dyeing techniques, they hired a talented weaver and dyer from Chinchero, a village near Cusco renowned for high-quality weaving and the use of plant-based dyes. This plant-dyed wool has been delivered to the family, and they have used these materials successfully to create textiles. This has inspired the Q'ewar founders to begin dyeing some wool cloth on-site for doll clothes, rather than purchasing chemically-dyed cloth.

Although the project philosophy espouses handwork done in community with others, in contrast to mass production or assembly line techniques, the project directors do not avoid the use of machines for some aspects of production. A

---

[3]Dyes based on aniline produce bright, long-lasting colors. However, exposure to aniline can cause adverse health effects, including methhemoglobinemia with acute exposure and liver, kidney, and spleen damage with chronic exposure. There is also some evidence of bladder tumors, but it is unclear whether exposure to aniline alone causes these tumors (U.S. Environmental Protection Agency [USEPA], 1994).

general rule is that the sewing of cloth, normally a two-dimensional activity, is done by machine, while much of the work with fibers, more of a three-dimensional process, is done by hand. As noted earlier, a hand-operated knitting machine has helped to facilitate the making of doll sweaters. The seamstresses for the Q'ewar Project use sewing machines, which they operate using a foot treadle. The clothing designer/seamstress for the large dolls operates an electrical machine in her home. Several of the workers stated that they prefer using the foot treadle machines as they can more easily control the speed. Sewing machines do provide for a higher quality of doll clothing because the machines produce more regular stitches. No one operating the machines is forced to work at a high speed. Julio and Lucy have purchased two new machines that they hope to integrate into the production process: one produces zigzag stitching and the other stitches borders.

Although Julio and Lucy prefer that women work together at the Q'ewar House, they also understand the need to work at home. For example, the clothing designer/seamstress for the large dolls asked to work at home, as her entire family is involved in the production process and her husband was not happy with her working outside her home. In addition, as mentioned above, many of the rural women who come on Saturday to spin alpaca fiber also knit doll clothes at home, and several other families weave doll ponchos and mantas at home. These people live too far away to travel to the Q'ewar House on a daily basis: for some, the walk takes up to 2½ hours. These women find time for this additional home work among the tasks of daily life such as farming, caring for children and animals, and preparing food.

Although each woman has responsibility for a specific aspect of doll making, some job rotation and variation does occur in the daily work. Julio and Lucy envision that eventually each worker will understand all aspects of the doll-making operation. The Q'ewar women often start work on one aspect of production and then learn another. For example they may begin by dyeing fabric and then learn to stuff and sew dolls. If a woman is not happy with a job to which she has been assigned she can request a different assignment. The exception to this practice is jobs that require training on machines, such as sewing and knitting; these specialized workers do not rotate frequently. Several of the Q'ewar workers rotate between doll making and working in the kitchen, where they prepare food for the children in the nursery and for Julio and Lucy.

The primary materials used to produce the Q'ewar dolls include cotton fabric, alpaca fiber and thread, sheep's wool, and a coarse cloth of sheep's wool called bayeta. The Q'ewar dolls are made using natural materials as much as possible. Julio and Lucy have a vision of producing a "100% organic" product, but this vision has been difficult to realize because they have encountered challenges in finding sources of organic cotton and naturally-dyed cloth.

Julio buys most of the materials locally that workers use to make Q'ewar dolls. He buys cotton fabric in Lima, 24 hours away by bus, or Arequipa, 12 hours away by bus. This cotton is produced industrially, and is not grown organically. On a global scale, Peru is only a minor producer of cotton.[4] Some Peruvian producers are beginning to produce organic cotton but they primarily export it to Europe where organic fibers command high prices. The Q'ewar Project has not yet found a domestic source for organic cotton. In addition, the variety of cotton fabric for doll clothing is limited as the domestic market favors synthetics that are less costly.

Julio buys alpaca fiber in an Andean town called Sicuani, a 4-hour bus trip away, where individuals bring alpaca fiber to market after they shear their animals during the warm, rainy months of November through March. Julio buys sheep's wool, bayeta cloth, and alpaca yarn from factories in Cusco, an hour by bus, and Juliaca, an 8-hour bus trip. The bayeta cloth and alpaca yarn are chemically dyed, using non-aniline dyes produced in Switzerland and the Netherlands. Other materials used in production include polyester thread, as cotton sewing thread can be almost impossible to find, along with cotton string, metal hooks, and buttons. These materials are purchased locally, but are produced in Mexico or China.

The Q'ewar doll-making process uses materials quite efficiently and produces very little waste. For example, if the alpaca fiber that is purchased for spinning turns out to have very short fibers, it will be used for stuffing dolls instead. If the spun thread is not of a quality suitable for doll hair, it will be used to knit sweaters or booties. Leftover cotton scraps are used to stuff pillows for the Q'ewar workshops. Other materials are also reused. For example, many materials are delivered in plastic sheeting that people find ways to reuse in other aspects of the production process. The alpaca yarn is laid out on the plastic sheeting after it has been washed, and the sheeting may also be used to carry materials needed for construction on the Q'ewar property. The women of Q'ewar take cotton scraps, plastic sheeting, and cardboard boxes for reuse in their homes. Very little accumulates as trash. Instead, people have a habit of creative reuse, as industrial materials are scarce.

Julio does not buy materials for doll production in large quantities because storage space is limited. In addition, moths can create problems if the materials are stored for a long time. Lavender flowers are grown at Q'ewar and used as a natural insect repellant, instead of using insecticides made from synthetic chemicals. An effort is made to send dolls to their destination as soon as orders are complete, to avoid insect problems. For this reason, only a limited stock of dolls, up to 200 at most, is kept on hand.

At present, the Q'ewar Project has no "doll hospital," unlike the American Girl company and Käthe Kruse doll company. Shipping costs would likely make this concept prohibitive. However, the project has made repairs when shipments arrived damaged. Once, for example, customs officials cut open some

---

[4] Six countries (China, United States, India, Pakistan, Uzbekistan, Egypt) account for 75% of the world's cotton output. See www.unctad.org

dolls when they saw the dark alpaca fiber inside and thought that drugs were being smuggled. Now the project uses only white alpaca fiber for doll stuffing.

HEALTH AND SAFETY ISSUES

Before working at the Q'ewar Project many of the women did physically taxing agricultural labor, and many still work in their fields each day before or after their work at the project. In contrast, Julio describes the production of Q'ewar dolls as a "rest" from physical labor. Still, in any work environment it is important to consider possible health and safety hazards. As discussed earlier, the workshops are well lit and clean. The women sit mostly on plastic chairs, made more comfortable with the addition of cloth pillows stuffed with alpaca fiber. The workers track the number of dolls needed for a particular order; still, the work pace always appeared to be relaxed and unhurried. Depending on the workshop, the tasks are varied; women can alternate between tasks such as stuffing dolls, sewing, and attaching hair.

Two issues are repetitive motion and fiber inhalation. Several of the jobs require repetitive motion. One woman spends much of her day unwinding balls of alpaca yarn, cleaning it, and rewinding the dried yarn back into balls. To do this, she uses a metal form that spins and allows her to unwind the yarn in large loops. This form requires continuous hand motion to keep it spinning. This worker acknowledged that her shoulder gets sore from this activity but said she had found ways to change position when she experienced discomfort and that the soreness subsided when she stopped. To reduce exposure to alpaca and cotton fibers, all the workers have been given dust masks, but most do not choose to wear them regularly. These masks do not prevent them from inhaling very small fibers, but may provide some protection from larger fibers. Overall, the work environment is kept clean and is ventilated through open doorways.

SPECIAL ASPECTS OF THE Q'EWAR PROJECT

The Q'ewar Project provides many benefits for its workers, including childcare, education, and healthcare. Lucy and Julio quickly realized that to participate fully in the doll-making operation, the Q'ewar workers needed on-site child-care. Their nursery is called Wawa Munakuy ("Giving love to the children" in Quechua) and provides for 15 children aged 6 months through 9 years. Two of the Q'ewar doll makers run the nursery. Julio and Lucy share a vision that this facility will become a Waldorf-inspired kindergarten. In 2005, Julio and Lucy hired a Waldorf teacher from Lima to begin the kindergarten program, but unfortunately this teacher was not a good match and did not stay with the project. Currently, Lucy is participating in a Waldorf education training course that is being held in Peru, Colombia, and Argentina in 6-week blocks over 2

Julio and Lucy, Q'ewar Project founders.

The Q'ewar workers on the patio of the Q'ewar House.

A variety of Q'ewar doll styles.

Spinning alpaca fiber.

Unwinding the alpaca yarn.

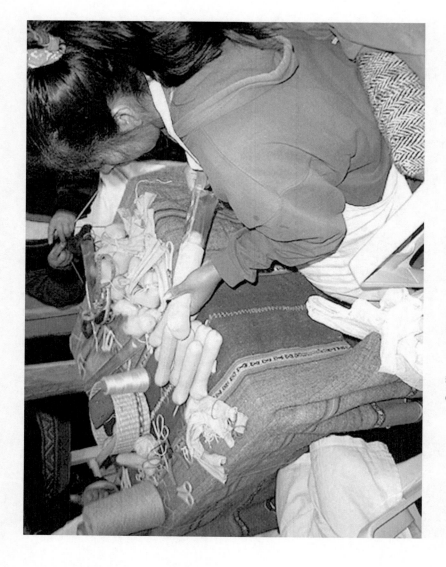

Stuffing a doll's leg by hand with sheep's wool.

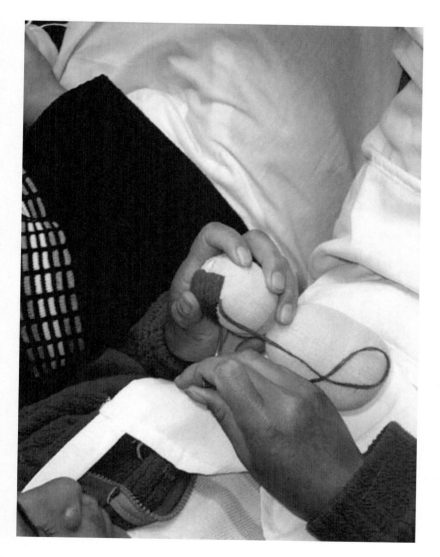

Sewing brown hair on medium doll.

Arms and legs are attached to body.

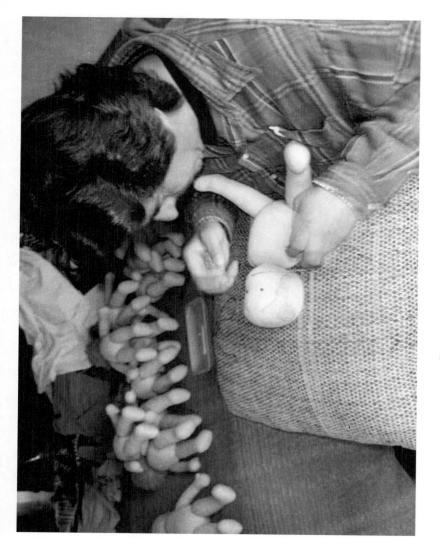

Eyes and mouth are hand-sewn.

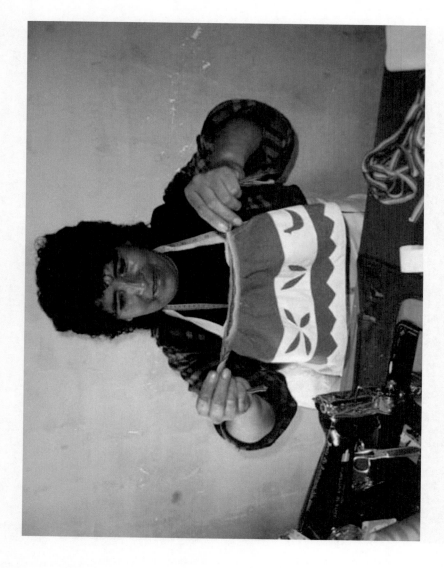

A "typical style" skirt.

The knitting machine.

Knitting workshop.

Sewing doll clothes with a foot treadle machine.

Dolls in garden.

Children returning from an outing.

Dolls and sweaters displayed in the Q'ewar shop.

years. Using this training, she plans to train Q'ewar workers so they can eventually take charge of the kindergarten. In 2007 workers began the construction of a new and larger schoolhouse for Wawa Munakuy.

Julio and Lucy also encourage the workers to attend training courses to learn new skills and augment their existing ones. Several of the women have attended sewing classes in a nearby town and they are receiving knitting instruction on-site. They are also offered instruction in literacy and basic computer skills. In addition, Lucy invites Quechua-speaking people who are engaged in community development to offer workshops on Saturday, including topics such as dental hygiene, sex education, and women's rights. The male Q'ewar workers have received instruction in auto mechanics and have learned how to drive a car. The Q'ewar Project funds these educational opportunities.

Julio and Lucy also make every effort to help address the health care needs of the Q'ewar workers, an important endeavor since free health care is not available and extreme poverty keeps 25% of Peruvians from having access to health care (Voice of America News, 2006). For example, one Q'ewar worker required extensive dental care after an infection and Julio and Lucy found doctors and a financial sponsor so that this health problem could be remedied. This assistance may extend to community members who are not Q'ewar workers or family members. A dog mauled a young boy in the community, and Julio and Lucy saw that his medical needs were addressed. This practice serves as an informal means of health insurance for the Q'ewar workers and is part of the couple's broader commitment to the social development of the community.

Other benefits include a garden, banking, bonuses, and community building. As noted earlier, the agricultural produce grown on the Q'ewar land is for the use of the Q'ewar workers and project directors. None is sold at a market. The workers can also take home plant material, such as dried corn stalks, to feed their animals.

Julio acts unofficially as a banker for many of the Q'ewar women. Rather than taking all of their earnings when they are paid each Saturday, many of the workers ask Julio to "save" some money for them. At the end of the calendar year, he gives them all of their savings. This process allows the women to save for larger expenditures; it may also give them more control over their income than turning it all over to their husbands, who may use it to purchase alcohol or other items that do not support the family. After one year of working at the Q'ewar Project, each worker receives a special one-time "gift" of approximately $150. This is a very large sum for an impoverished family in Peru and Julio and Lucy hope that the women will use this money for some needed home repair or household item.

Finally, several times a year special outings are planned to take the Q'ewar women to visit local sites such as Incan ruins or hot springs. Many of the workers have never been to these sites. These outings provide opportunities for community building, rest and relaxation, and cultural education.

THE ECONOMICS OF THE Q'EWAR PROJECT

The Q'ewar Project directors are proud that the project is self-sustaining. In 2007 the project's annual expenses totaled approximately $100,000. Expenses include labor, materials, travel to purchase materials, shipping and insurance costs, and retail store expenses. Less directly related to doll production are costs for construction, the garden, and the yearly outings, and special celebrations. The project also covers living expenses for Julio and Lucy, who do not receive salaries for their work. In this context, donations of equipment such as the sewing and knitting machine have greatly assisted the project.

The workers of the Q'ewar Project produced approximately 1,000 dolls in 2005 and 2,000 in 2007. Because the project faces competition from other companies and organizations making similar Waldorf-style dolls, Julio and Lucy price the dolls somewhat lower than their competitors. In 2006 the Q'ewar Project received $55 to $60 for each large doll and $20 for the medium dolls. Each doll seller in the United States and Europe can set her or his own prices for the dolls and keep any profit made to cover marketing expenses, or return all the profit to the Q'ewar Project. In 2007 doll sales generated approximately $87,000. With donations, the 2007 project income was approximately $140,000.

Given the narrow margin between income and expenses, marketing is important. In both the United States and Europe, the dolls are distributed by volunteers who have learned of the Q'ewar Project and want to support it. Waldorf school stores and fairs are still the primary sales venue, but provide a relatively small customer base. The dolls are increasingly being sold at stores that support "fair trade." In addition, the Nova Natural company features the Q'ewar dolls in its catalog as their Waldorf Doll offering and hopes to eventually sell 500 of them a year. The dolls are also sold at a farmers' market in Minnesota and at a thrift store in Vermont.

Q'ewar dolls are sold in two locations in Peru. The first is a shop that opened on the main square of Andahuaylillas in 2004. The shop is strategically located next to the famous colonial church on the square known as the "Sistine Chapel of the Americas" because of its painted ceiling and ornate decoration. Many tour buses stop briefly to let tourists view the church. There is a small local market on the square and many tourists also visit the Q'ewar Project shop. Four women work in the shop creating the bambino dolls, answering tourist inquiries, and selling dolls along with other Peruvian products such as sweaters, hats, and purses made in Juliaca and other locations.

The Q'ewar dolls are also sold at the exclusive Hotel Monasterio in Cusco, where they can be beautifully displayed in the hotel's upscale shop. The shop's operator is involved with the Peruvian Waldorf community and carries the dolls to support the project. The project directors are concerned that others will make cheap copies of the dolls, which could undermine the project, so they carefully consider where the dolls will be sold in Peru.

A key element in marketing the dolls is the Q'ewar Web site (www.qewar.com), which provides a detailed history of the project and includes many photos of the doll-making operation. In addition, each doll is sold with an informative tag that describes the project's social development intent. Beyond these efforts, the Q'ewar Project directors do not get directly involved in marketing the dolls. They leave this activity to the doll distributors, who often create displays to educate potential consumers about the project. Although many aspects of the doll are environmentally friendly, the Q'ewar doll is not marketed as such. Instead, the marketing focuses on the project's efforts to help these rural women. It also highlights the originality of the dolls and the use of local materials such as alpaca and bayeta.

In 2007 the Q'ewar women workers received approximately $5.60 per day. When the project began in 2002, the starting wage was approximately $2 per day. Julio and Lucy determined the daily rate after learning that this was an average wage for village women working in other jobs. Wages have risen as doll sales have increased. A full-time Q'ewar doll maker receives approximately $140 per month, which is below the official minimum wage of $155 (U.S. Department of State, 2008). Typically, a minimum wage is set by a government for workers in the formal sector and is determined in an urban context. However, the Q'ewar Project is part of the informal sector, and rural costs of living are different from those in Peruvian cities. In addition, the Q'ewar workers receive produce from the Q'ewar garden at no cost, have on-site childcare at low cost, and receive medical assistance as needed.

The women who come on Saturday to spin alpaca fiber are paid approximately $3.75 per day for their efforts. They may also take alpaca fiber home with them to spin when they have time; they receive $6/kilo for this effort. They can also take home alpaca fiber that is not suitable for spinning, but needs to be carded; for this task, they receive approximately $3/kilo.

The two skilled designers/seamstresses for the Q'ewar Project each receive approximately $300 per month. One of these workers is funded through a Swiss foundation and the other is paid directly by the Q'ewar Project. The men who work for the Q'ewar Project receive roughly $5 to $8 per day, the teenaged workers receiving less than the experienced construction workers.

When I asked Julio if workers receive a fair wage, he responded that the Q'ewar Project seeks to pay its workers more than the average wage and aims to raise wages as more income comes into the project. One worker responded that the wage is a living wage "if you are careful about how you spend your money." This worker is married and her income supplements that of her husband. However, many of the Q'ewar workers are unmarried and no one else in their household contributes any income. The wages earned at the Q'ewar project allow these workers to meet basic needs such as having electricity in their homes. Most village residents also have animals for milk and small farm plots that provide necessities such as corn and potatoes.

The International Fair Trade Association (IFAT), a global network of fair trade organizations, describes a key principle of fair trade as "payment of a fair price." This means that the price of the product "covers not only the cost of production but enables production which is socially just and environmentally sound. It provides fair pay to the producers and takes into account the principle of equal pay for equal work by women and men."[5]

Julio defines fair trade somewhat differently, as eliminating intermediaries and ensuring that producers and sellers share the profits. When setting prices for the Q'ewar dolls, he accounts for all of the labor and materials that go into production, but also looks to set a price that is competitive with other similar dolls on the market. As noted above, the doll distributors pay the Q'ewar Project a set price for each doll, but can also choose to return more money to the project by setting higher doll prices and/or returning more of the profit.

NEW DIRECTIONS FOR THE Q'EWAR PROJECT

The Q'ewar Project directors are considering expanding production to include clothing and sculpture. Shawls and sweaters for adults are already being produced on a small scale, but the workers need to improve their knitting skills to meet the precision and quality requirements of the world market. Sizing requirements are different for European consumers who prefer narrower, longer clothes; Peruvian patterns tend to be wider and shorter. Shawls are currently sold in the United States and Europe and sweaters are sold in Europe only. Baby clothes are being considered; the initial design under development is an outfit for newborns that would include a one-piece suit, cap, booties, and receiving blanket. Finally, Julio plans to begin teaching wood sculpture to the Q'ewar workers and other residents of Andahuaylillas. He is considering using the second floor of the Q'ewar shop in the town plaza as a location for a gallery where sculptural works could be exhibited and sold.

Julio and Lucy hope to eventually train the Q'ewar workers more broadly in the various aspects of the production process and to gradually increase the responsibilities of those workers who exhibit leadership capabilities. Through their dedication and charismatic leadership, the Q'ewar Project has developed and grown over the last 6 years. Their deep commitment to serve others is very evident. As Lucy told me, "this is what feeds the project." The challenge for the future is evident: to develop this project so that it will be self-sustaining, even when Julio and Lucy retire from their leadership roles.

[5] http://www.ifat.org/index.php?option=com_content&task=view&id=2&Itemid=14

CHAPTER 7

Emerging Themes for Sustainable Product Design

According to the *New York Times* columnist Nicholas Kristof, "industrialization in its early stages is always clothed in wretchedness" (Kristof & WuDunn, 2000, p. 119). Although occupational and environmental hazards are often dismissed as necessary steps on the path to modernization, it is important to ask whether this model of globalization and industrialization is really the only way forward, or whether other paths to development are also viable.

The work environments of the Käthe Kruse doll company and Q'ewar Project let us envision alternatives to the dominant model of low-wage, high-stress assembly-line toy production under inhumane and hazardous conditions. Although the Käthe Kruse company and the Q'ewar Project are small-scale operations compared to large multi-national toy companies, their product designs, materials choices, and work environments provide a vision of a more humane system that is also gentler to the earth. These examples of successful, healthy alternatives provide useful information to counter the predominant paradigm.

When considered against the five elements of sustainable product design that provided the underlying conceptual and organizing framework for this study, none of the dolls studied fully exemplify sustainable design. Yet each case tells an important story and reveals something that is vital to consider in the pursuit of sustainable product design. Table 1 provides a summary of my findings from three case studies relative to the elements of sustainable product design (in the Appendix, Tables 1–3 provide supplementary information). In addition, as I synthesized this research, five key themes emerged: care, human dignity, intention, materials choices, and transparency. In the rest of this chapter, I compare the three cases and then consider the five themes. I also discuss economic challenges to implementing sustainable product design.

Table 1. Summary of Sustainable Design Elements for Three Case Studies

Sustainable Product Design Elements	American Girl/Mattel	Käthe Kruse doll company	Q'ewar Project
SAFE for workers	Conditions at American Girl headquarters, distribution centers, and retail stores are likely to meet criteria, but employees in production facilities overseas work long hours at low wages. Hours and pace are excessive; employees do not have adequate health and safety training or PPE; chemicals used in production present hazards to workers; and some dormitory conditions are unsatisfactory.	Workplace is clean and well lit.	The Q'ewar Project work environment is safe for workers. Health hazards are minimal.
		Workers have some control over daily activities.	
			Aniline dyes are used in the making of doll ponchos and shawls—this occurs off-site and is being phased out.
		Craft production—pace and hours are not excessive.	
		Workers receive health and safety training.	
	Workers do not have freedom of association.	Chemicals used in polyurethane, polystyrene, and vinyl production present hazards to workers.	
	Workers do not have job control or input into production process.	Workers in industrial cotton production face chemical and other hazards; sourcing of organic cotton will reduce these hazards.	
	Workers in industrial cotton and textile production face chemical and other hazards.		
	Mattel is enforcing rules against child labor.		

HEALTHY for consumers	Dolls are developmentally appropriate. Dolls meet European and American safety standards.	Dolls are developmentally appropriate. Dolls meet European and American safety standards. Cloth dolls use high quality Öko-Tex certified textiles, which are safe for the consumer.	This product is healthy for consumers—doll is developmentally appropriate, soft, safe, made of natural materials.
ENVIRONMENTALLY sound	Dolls are durable, repairable, and can be disassembled—doll hospital is important product-service system. Plastic waste is reused in injection molding. Some petroleum-based solvents have been replaced by water-based solvents. Some packaging is environmentally preferable. Chemicals used in vinyl production are hazardous to the environment. Industrial cotton production is hazardous to ecosystems. Industrial wool production uses hazardous chemicals. Plastic dolls are not recyclable.	Cloth dolls use Öko-Tex 100 certified textiles. Dolls are durable, repairable, and can be disassembled. Materials diversity is minimized, renewable resources used. Waste is minimized. Chemicals used in polyurethane, polystyrene, and vinyl production are hazardous to the environment. Industrial cotton production is hazardous to ecosystems. Sourcing of organic cotton will reduce this hazard. Wool production uses hazardous chemicals.	Natural, renewable materials used, and production is on a small scale so that materials are not used at rate greater than regenerative capacity. Aniline dyes used in one aspect of production process—goal is to eliminate in favor of plant dyes.

Table 1. (Cont'd.)

Sustainable Product Design Elements	American Girl/Mattel	Käthe Kruse doll company	Q'ewar Project
ENVIRONMENTALLY sound (cont'd.)	Millions of catalogs are distributed annually. Efforts are being made to use more recycled paper and target audience for catalogs. Mattel 2007 Global Citizenship report notes 38% reduction in energy consumption in its Bangkok factory by improving preventive maintenance systems.	Plastic dolls are not recyclable. Öko-Tex 100 certified textiles are not necessarily produced in an environmentally sound way, but some factories have Öko-Tex 1000 certification to indicate eco-friendly production practices.	
BENEFICIAL to local communities	Financial donations from American Girl and Pleasant Rowland have greatly benefited the Madison Arts community, environmental education efforts, and other nonprofit organizations in the United States. Profits from doll sales have not directly benefited the communities in which the dolls are made.	Company has longevity in community—60 years. Supportive to family life—flexible work hours, ability to leave company and return part-time. Wages are average for textile industry.	Project is designed to empower community and is providing a sustainable livelihood. Profits are reinvested in community. Work design promotes community input and participation.

ECONOMICALLY viable		
American Girl company sales have risen over 20 years, in contrast to declining sales of Barbie.	Company in existence for 100 years; in Donauwörth for 60 years—recent diversification of product lines indicates that company is branching out to stay competitive.	Project is stable in its philosophy.
Price of doll does not internalize social and environmental production costs.	Low worker turnover and high satisfaction with work environment.	Profits are reinvested.
Detailed data on revenues/sales/costs of production are not available.	Environmental and social costs are not fully internalized.	Employees are well utilized.
		Communication is valued.
		Difficult to know whether this product will be economically viable for the long-term because of possibly limited market for this doll.
		Unclear whether innovation will be sufficient to meet market requirements.

COMPARING THE CASE STUDIES

As described in depth in chapter 4, two major factors account for the success of the American Girl company: a unique design which gives preteen girls a compelling alternative to a Barbie doll or a baby doll; and brilliant marketing through catalogs, a Web site, magazine, and retail locations. Founder Pleasant Rowland had a great desire to teach "living history" to preteen girls through books and an accompanying character doll. This concept resulted in a financial success on a scale she might not have imagined at the outset. The "razor/razor blade" approach of selling dolls, accompanied by doll clothing, accessories, and books has yielded tremendous profit.[1] The American Girl doll has proven profitable for Mattel even as sales of their iconic product, Barbie, are lagging.

When judged by traditional business standards, the rise of the American Girl company is a classic American success story. Pleasant Rowland started with passion, a unique concept, and enough personal funds to capitalize the business. The product took off and 13 years later was purchased by Mattel, which recognized the profitability of adding this niche product to its array of toy offerings. The American Girl company is understandably proud of its financial success— as exemplified in part by the expansion of its "entertainment retail" locations. However, this model of economic success is shaky at best from the perspective of long-term sustainability. When analyzed according to the five elements of sustainable product design, the American Girl doll meets only two of the five elements. The product is healthy and developmentally appropriate for the consumer and it has proven to be economically viable. But this economical viability is built on the low-wage labor of young Chinese women and the externalization of environmental and social costs. Hidden behind the success of this product is the company's failure to address the other three elements of sustainable product design. When I asked to interview Pleasant Rowland for this study to learn about her original doll design (she ultimately declined to speak with me), her assistant said, "How is the American Girl doll sustainable? After all, it's made of vinyl." The company does not question the use of toxic inputs such as polyvinyl chloride, petroleum-based solvents, and paints, as its business strategy does not include a precautionary approach to the use of toxic materials. Production is outsourced to locations where health, safety, and environmental laws are routinely violated. Mattel, the world's largest toy company and the owner of the American Girl company, has taken leadership in the toy industry to improve working conditions in its own and vendor factories around the world, but so far has had limited success. The corporate philanthropy of Pleasant Rowland and the American Girl company has greatly benefited

[1] This marketing principle was first perfected by Mattel for Barbie dolls. Just as the owner of a razor needs razor blades, the doll owner "needs" accessories and additional clothing for meaningful play (Cross & Smits, 2005).

communities in the United States, but this generosity does not extend to the locations in China where the dolls are produced.

The dolls made by the Käthe Kruse company, described in chapter 5, are further on the continuum toward sustainable product design. This company, with approximately 800 employees, has a different philosophy than that of a large publicly owned multinational corporation. The company must meet certain financial goals but is less driven by the need for short-term profits because it does not answer to shareholders. The owners are attuned to the financial bottom line, but also bring other values to their decision making. Foremost is preserving the quality of the product and maintaining the century-old Käthe Kruse brand. For this reason, the company has continued to create traditional Käthe Kruse doll designs for serious adult doll collectors. These dolls, handcrafted with exquisite detail, are very expensive and are not a typical toy for children.

To stay competitive in the children's toy market, in recent years the company has innovated by introducing a highly successful line of Waldorf-style cloth dolls. One could infer from this choice to pursue eco-friendly design in these dolls and other toys that this is a primary value of the company. However, the owners have also developed a line of lower-cost vinyl dolls that are made in China but are still recognizable as the Käthe Kruse brand. The owner says they are producing dolls made of PVC because consumers prefer a more durable, less breakable doll. The lower costs for these dolls reflect the significantly lower costs of labor and materials and the externalization of the environmental and social costs of producing the dolls. In our interviews, both the company owner and the purchasing agent acknowledged their concerns about working conditions in China and indicated they had some discomfort with outsourcing any large portion of production to Asian factories.

The Käthe Kruse doll company is notable for its materials choices. Of the textiles it purchases for doll and clothing production, 99% are certified to the Öko-Tex Standard 100, an eco-label that is well recognized in Europe. This standard is designed to protect the consumer of the textile as the finished fabric must not contain toxic residues. This label does not ensure that the textile was produced in an environmentally sustainable manner, but is a step in the right direction.

The dolls of the Käthe Kruse doll company meet many of the sustainable product design elements in that they are healthy for the consumer, beneficial to the local community, and financially viable. For over a century, the company has continued to produce a high-quality product and has continually innovated to stay competitive. The company has remained in Donauwörth, Germany, for over 50 years and has provided stable and flexible employment for a primarily female workforce. In recent years the owners have outsourced 90% of production to a factory in Latvia. By regionalizing production in Latvia rather than outsourcing production to factories in China, the company can better control product quality and can also ensure the quality of the work environment. The Käthe Kruse doll company owns the Latvian factory and the owners have hired a trusted production manager.

However, the product is not completely safe for workers to produce, nor is it fully environmentally sound. As noted above, the owners do not question the use of toxic inputs in the production process. They choose to use vinyl, which is hazardous to produce and dispose of, because of its durability and low cost. Two other hazardous materials, polystyrene and polyurethane, are used in the production of the classic dolls; polystyrene is used to make doll heads at an off-site factory and polyurethane is used on-site to produce foam doll bodies. The company continues to make these toys because a market exists for them; it does not intend to eliminate toxic chemicals from the production process. Yet, European regulations are beginning to drive some materials choices. For example, the company requires certification from Asian factories that the vinyl doll parts do not contain phthalates above the limits set by the European Union and it conducts laboratory tests to ensure that limits are met.

The Q'ewar Project beautifully illustrates a model that puts workers, consumers, the environment, and the local community ahead of profits. These dolls exemplify many elements of sustainable product design. The design and production of these dolls are significantly different from those of either Käthe Kruse or American Girl. As the Q'ewar Project is not a typical business enterprise, these cases are not directly comparable. The vision of the Q'ewar Project is of social development for individuals and eventually for the entire community of Andahuaylillas, located in the Peruvian Andes. Human dignity is the cornerstone on which this effort rests. The work environment is designed to engage and empower workers through the making of "social art." The design of both the product and work environment is intentional. The doll is designed to be developmentally appropriate for young children and to use safe, natural, and local materials, while the work environment is designed to be safe, healthy, and nurturing for the workers. At this point in the evolution of the project, aniline dyes, which can be harmful to humans and the environment, are still used in preparing some wool fibers. But the project directors have begun to eliminate these toxic chemicals from the production process by hiring an expert in plant-based dyeing techniques.

The fifth element of sustainable product design, that of economic viability, remains an open question for the Q'ewar Project. Its annual income from doll sales is only slightly higher than its annual expenses. The project has achieved much success since it was initiated in 2002 and is operating in the black to date. All profits are returned to the project by increasing salaries for workers or building additional workshop space. Although the project directors are innovating with new products, to date the market niche for these products is quite small. To survive in the long run, the project will need to expand its market beyond the Waldorf school communities in the United States and Europe. The project founders have begun to do this by marketing their dolls as "fairly traded." This is still a niche market but it offers additional locales for doll sales.

I now turn to the themes that emerged out of this research.

THE SIGNIFICANCE OF CARE

Because dolls are replicas of the human form they are easy to love; we are not surprised when children attribute human qualities to these objects. As dolls are deeply cared for by both child and adult consumers, they are ideal objects for considering the value of "care." The *American Heritage Dictionary* defines care as "an object of attention or solicitude, caution, heedfulness, protection, attentiveness to detail, painstaking application, conscientiousness" (Morris, 1969). In this section I consider attentiveness and solicitude toward the doll being produced as well as the worker creating the object for sale. What is the value of a product made with care—to workers, consumers, and the earth? Does the design of the work environment influence whether a product can be made with care? Can a product made with care help teach consumers about conserving it and the resources with which it was made?

Two of the three cases illustrate craft production of dolls and the other case illustrates mass production on an assembly line. To many in the business world, craft production has become an anachronism for all but a narrow niche of high-end products because of its relatively slow pace, high expense, and its need for skilled workers. In the early 1900s Frederick Taylor and others expounded their theories of "scientific management" and began a revolution in production techniques that has continued to this day. This approach to mass production, first popularized by Henry Ford, emphasized simplifying tasks through the use of machines, standardized parts design, and the progressive assembly line. These changes in the work environment, in addition to increasing efficiency, allowed management to wrest control from highly skilled craft workers. This work design allowed products to be produced on a mass scale but created a work environment that was deskilled, repetitive, fast-paced, and stressful for workers. This is the type of work environment found at a typical toy factory in southern China.

In these factories "quality" trumps "care." Quality applies to the end product and is not about the design of the work environment. Managers review quality to ensure that the product consistently meets a set of specifications. For example, Mattel's Chang-an plant has been recognized as a "World Quality Manager," as it adopted "just in time" strategies.[2] In this factory workers may be punished for failing to produce products of sufficient quality (Wong & Frost, 2000). A recent

---

[2]Automobile manufacturers such as Subaru have adopted lean production and "just in time" strategies. The results of research in these large manufacturing settings demonstrate that lean production has reduced worker control, has not greatly increased the thinking component of the work, and has increased psychosocial stress and risk of illnesses and injuries, in particular, musculoskeletal disorders (Graham, 1995).

audit report by the International Center for Corporate Accountability noted that at one plant "workers are required to reimburse the factory for the cost of materials lost whenever the defect rate at the assembly line exceeds 2%. The report states that "workers are being unfairly penalized . . . for a management problem" (ICCA, 2006b, p. 51).

This focus on quality ignores the worker. Although "quality control" is an important part of the production process, making a product with "care" is not a significant part of the equation. In a work environment where the worker is not cared for, it is unlikely that the worker can care for the product she is producing. When a company focuses on quality over care, both the workers and the product suffer the consequences. As the many toy recalls of 2007 revealed, quality control may also be compromised in a work environment where cost-cutting is valued above all. Leaded paint and toxic glues were substituted for safer materials in production, at least in part because of their lower cost (Barboza, 2007; Bradsher, 2007).

Craft production, as practiced in Germany at the Käthe Kruse doll company and in Peru at the Q'ewar Project, provides a sharp contrast to the monotonous, fast-paced, and high-stress assembly-line production of dolls in Asian factories. In both Germany and Peru, workers are not merely cogs in a wheel. Instead, they are engaged in making a whole doll rather than the same part over and over again. This approach of making the whole rather than one part has also been implemented in other sectors to increase work satisfaction and quality; examples are quality circles and self-managing teams at automotive factories (Volvo, 2005). The workers express pride in their handiwork. The care that is imbued in this process of craft production is transmitted in an intangible way to the product. For example, as one worker in Germany carried a box of partially constructed dolls from the "doll stuffing" workshop to the room where wigs are attached and dolls are dressed, she said "I've come to get the kids." These products, made with care, do take on an almost human quality.

At the Q'ewar Project in Peru, making a product with care is recognized as having spiritual significance. Julio and Lucy, the founders, describe how the spiritual aspects of a human being are tapped as they do artistic work in community with others. The doll maker becomes an intermediary who transmits this spiritual intention through the doll to the consumer, a child. Julio and Lucy believe that an unhappy worker cannot create a doll that will be healthy for a child. Therefore, they pay great attention to the physical, emotional, and spiritual health of the workers. This is one reason that high-quality childcare is provided on-site, as the founders understand that the workers cannot attend to their work if they are worrying about the safety of their children. Also, workers who have been victims of domestic violence receive counseling and support as part of their participation in the project. The ethic of care in producing the product imbues it with a value beyond a monetary one. It influences the design of the work itself, as the work-place nurtures an environment of care for both the product and the workers.

This caring approach also provides an opportunity to recognize the natural and human resources that went into making the object. For example, Käthe Kruse classic dolls are stuffed with reindeer hair and have human hair wigs. The Peruvian dolls are made from alpaca fiber and sheep's wool, both grown locally. These are unusual materials, native to certain parts of the world. As consumers come to know about products that are made with care, from the perspective of both the workers who make them and the materials that are used, they may be more likely to value and conserve them, rather than treat them as many products are handled today—as common, cheap, and disposable.

All of these cases illustrate dolls that are meant to be cared for over time. They are meant to be "objects of attention and solicitude," rather than throwaway toys. They are durable and repairable. Both American Girl and Käthe Kruse offer a "doll hospital" to repair "injured" dolls. The American Girl company has been successful in connecting "caring" for the doll with the purchase of additional doll accessories. The company's clever marketing strategies—using its catalogs, Web site, and retail locations—effectively relay a strong message that the dolls "need" a variety of outfits and accessories for successful play and that one doll is not enough. In affluent communities, girls often have two, three, or even four American Girl dolls.

It is ironic that the American Girl doll, made in factories where care for the workers is not a priority, can so successfully market "caring" for the doll, as well as "caring" for the preteen girl, through the company's many advice books for girls. This compartmentalized "caring" ignores the conditions under which these dolls were produced.

How can we as consumers begin to care for the worker who creates the object as well as for the child for whom we purchase the object? The American Girl doll is seen by many middle-class progressive parents as a healthy alternative to a fashion doll such as Barbie. For those who do not know the details of its production, it stands out as a preferable, alternative choice. A young child who is the ultimate consumer of this product may not be able to recognize the environmental and social costs of its production. The adult caretaker of the child, however, who is usually the purchaser of this product, has a different relationship with this object. As adults, consumers, and citizens of the world, once we understand the embedded history of a product, we have the ability to act, both to educate others and to create pressure to improve conditions for the workers who make our toys and many other consumer products.

The theme of care has obvious connections to the second theme, of human dignity.

DESIGNING WORK FOR HUMAN DIGNITY

The cases studied here present a spectrum: from the Peruvian Q'ewar Project's cottage-based production, where groups of four women work together creating

dolls primarily by hand; to the Käthe Kruse doll company's craft production that
is a mix of mechanized and hand labor, also done in small workshops; and finally,
to the mass production of the American Girl doll on assembly lines of 5,000 to
10,000 workers in factories in southern China. These production processes in
Germany and Peru are models of "conducive production," where work design
involves a broad recombination of skills, is nonhierarchical, and asks workers to
take responsibility for coordinating their own jobs (Karasek, 1999).

The importance of having some job control and flexibility cannot be overstated.
Workers who can manage their job tasks with some independence will shift from
one aspect of production to another to avoid monotony and also to avoid injury
or pain. At the Käthe Kruse workshop, workers cope with discomfort by shifting
to another aspect of their job, thereby reducing strain on a particular body part
or set of muscles. Workers commonly develop such strategies to avoid pain;
women with repetitive, boring jobs are more likely to develop musculo-skeletal
disorders than other workers (Messing, 1998). Workers at the Käthe Kruse doll
company in Germany described how quality trumped speed; although they had
quotas they were supposed to meet, they had some flexibility in meeting these
goals as long as they maintained the high quality of production.

The conditions for high stress are found in large toy factories in China: during
peak season the production demand is high but workers have little control over
their work environment (Karasek, 1992). In contrast, the level of stress in the
work environments in the Germany and Peru cases appears to be relatively low.
Although workers at the Käthe Kruse doll company experience high demands at
certain times in the production cycle, they have autonomy in determining how to
do the job, which may moderate stress. In addition, workers are cross-trained
so that they understand many aspects of the production process and can participate
in a range of activities. This increases production efficiency and at the same time
reduces monotony for them. At the Q'ewar Project in Peru, the pace of work is
moderate, and priority is given to ensuring a humane work environment, with
workers participating in the design of the work process. In both these cases,
workers have high "decision latitude," so that even at times of high demand, they
are able to work comfortably and can moderate job stress (Karasek, 1992).

A flexible work environment indicates respect for human dignity, as it
acknowledges the holistic nature of people's lives, which includes their families
and other commitments outside the work environment. At the Käthe Kruse
company, the work hours are flexible to accommodate mothers with children
and the company is "family-friendly," allowing employees to leave their jobs
for extended periods while they are raising their children and then offering
opportunities to return part- or full-time. Most of the employees I interviewed
had been with the company more than ten years and many had returned after
taking time off to raise their children.

At the Q'ewar Project, workers also rotate among different jobs, including
work in the nursery and kitchen as well as doll production. Workers can request a

different job assignment if they are not satisfied with their current assignment, without fear of reprisal. As noted earlier, workers can bring their children with them to the Q'ewar House, as they have access to high-quality childcare on-site. The project directors have also recognized the need to assist in supporting sustainable livelihoods for the men of the community and have employed five male workers in agriculture and construction at the Q'ewar House. Plans are underway for a sculpture workshop that will employ additional men in the village.

The features of the work environment described above support the dignity and well-being of the worker. Because of the small scale of the operation, the Q'ewar Project can attend to the needs and concerns of individuals. This is more difficult to accomplish in a larger-scale operation. The Käthe Kruse doll company has approximately 85 workers at its headquarters in Donauwörth, Germany, and 700 in its factory in Latvia. Workers told me that the calmness and flexibility that was evident in Donauwörth carried over to the Latvian operation. Also, children of Latvian workers are allowed to come to the factory after school and a place is available for them to do their homework.

China is undergoing a massive industrial revolution that is creating a large consumer class and slowly raising living standards for many of its citizens. This can be viewed positively from a macro economic perspective. But, as described in detail in chapter 4, the work environment of a typical toy factory in southern China is not designed to respect human dignity. Although Mattel is working to improve working conditions by implementing its Global Manufacturing Principles, these incremental improvements do not change the basic paradigm embodied in this work design, which values economic return to shareholders over worker rights or community needs.

Researchers have begun to analyze how the shift to a market economy is affecting rural Chinese communities and are documenting the social impacts of these changes (Dunn, 2006). Writing in the *Washington Post*, Peter Goodman (2006) described how serving as the "factory for the world" has had tremendous social costs on individual lives and communities. One migrant worker may be able to raise an entire family out of poverty. However, this means family members are separated, as factories are not designed to support community and family life. Young female workers are frequently forced to leave their children to be raised by grandparents in rural villages. Most workers can afford to visit their home village only once a year, at the New Year when factories typically close for 5 days. This has fragmented family relationships. Goodman (2006) reported on the situation of a woman named Li Meilan, who has left her 5-year-old son behind in the village of Tanqui with her mother-in-law for most of his life while she and her husband run a small business in Guangdong. "My son refuses to call me mother." He calls me "older sister," and says, "you're not my mother." It's a very bad feeling" (para. 9).

Factory workers share their income with their family back in their home village, to help improve the material status of family members. This often means that migrant workers are desperate for factory jobs and will continue working there under the worst of conditions. Said a Shenzhen factory worker, "It's better to have bad conditions than no job at all" (Goldman, 2004, para. 16).

Situations like this, which leave a worker desperate for a job, even one with bad conditions, offer a challenge to those who would develop a vision of sustainability.

INTENTION AND VISION FOR SUSTAINABILITY

Sustainability expert Lorinda Rowledge and her colleagues describe how a revolution in thinking and knowledge is needed to attain a revolution in action on sustainability. They describe several of the key elements of this new paradigm. We will need simultaneous solutions to economic, environmental, and social goals rather than seeing them as trade-offs. We will need life-cycle thinking, management and responsibility, closed loop systems, and ways to build prevention principles into product design. Finally, and perhaps most challenging, economic growth must be decoupled from environmental resource use (Rowledge, Barton, & Brady, 1999, p. 35). In the foreword to their book, John Elkington, a sustainability expert from the United Kingdom, delineates several key characteristics of companies that have committed to a sustainability agenda. He says they have a clear and focused strategic perspective on how sustainability relates to the company, its value chains, markets, products, and operations. Their management systems enable the company to monitor and manage environmental and social issues and integrate them into core business decisions. Their product development processes integrate triple-bottom-line thinking (considering economic prosperity, environmental quality, and social equity as equally important) into the design process and account for impacts throughout the life cycle. In their innovative supply chain management approaches, they see the environmental and social performance of their suppliers as an important part of their company's overall performance. They also require open, transparent, quantified, and verified communication of their triple-bottom-line performance (Rowledge et al., pp. 13–14). Thus, a commitment to a sustainability agenda begins with intention and vision and requires effective leadership. In large organizations, this intention must be put into practice by strategically planning and developing goals and practical action plans, as well as employee training and incentives for participation, along with systems for measurement, reporting, and accountability. In small organizations, charismatic leadership and commitment may be sufficient to carry through a vision of sustainability.

What is the sustainability intention and vision of those providing leadership in the three cases studied for this research project? Does it provide a revolution in thinking and knowledge as described above that can lead to action and change? The Q'ewar Project leadership provides an example of vision and intention that is driving both the design of the product and the design of the work environment. Above all, the Q'ewar Project founders value human dignity, which deeply influences how the work is organized and how workers are treated. In addition, the project envisions a 100% organic, natural doll made of local materials. This goal is close to being achieved, except for the doll ponchos and shawls, which are dyed with aniline dyes. Because of the directors' intention, the organization is moving toward realizing this objective by hiring an expert in plant dyeing. Because of the primary value placed on human dignity and social development the Q'ewar directors have chosen to continue to work with the family that uses the aniline dyes rather than exclude them, as the family is dependent on this work for their livelihood. The founder's goal is to educate this family and provide them with plant-dyed fibers so that they will no longer need to use chemical dyes.

In contrast, at the Käthe Kruse doll company, economic factors drive decision making more than an explicit company philosophy of sustainability. However, the company owners are committed to upholding the quality of the Käthe Kruse brand through craft production of their products and have maintained a flexible and supportive work environment. The company's decision to produce both eco-friendly cloth dolls and vinyl dolls was a calculated strategy to remain competitive with other toy companies by offering similar product choices. Although the company does not embrace a precautionary approach to chemical use as a strategic priority, European regulations and eco-labeling opportunities are driving safer product design.

What is the vision and intention of the American Girl company in terms of sustainability?[3] Its mission is simply to "celebrate girls," and the company has succeeded greatly in honoring girlhood through its books, which are peopled with courageous, responsible, and intelligent young heroines and the dolls that represent these characters. Mattel's Corporate Social Responsibility Report states that "globalization of opportunity should be accompanied by globalization of responsibility," acknowledging that Mattel has an obligation to "have a positive impact on the people and places we touch" (Mattel, 2003a, p. 3). Mattel has taken leadership to improve working conditions in Chinese factories. It also participates in the Global Reporting Initiative (GRI), a program to improve corporate reporting and accountability on economic, social, and environmental performance.[4] Mattel is to be commended for participating in these efforts. Yet a close reading of their GRI report reveals statements such as "Mattel's products and operations do not have impacts on the biodiversity of our environment" and "Mattel's products have a relatively insignificant environmental impact" (Mattel, 2003b, pp. 18–19). If this is truly the perspective of company management, it does not indicate an understanding of the global implications of their operations or a particularly forward-looking business strategy in terms

---

[3] The American Girl company is a wholly owned subsidiary of Mattel.
[4] See www.globalreporting.org

of sustainability. Mattel uses the language of sustainability to describe its efforts in product development, supply chain management, and management systems. But a review of its efforts in these realms reveals a company just beginning to move beyond environmental compliance rather than one with a strategic vision of sustainability. Mattel's efforts to implement its Global Manufacturing Principles focus on correcting problems within the current paradigm of industrialization and globalization. This approach is likely to result in incremental changes in the existing system rather than making the radical changes that are needed.

What would it take to move toward truly sustainable design of products?

CHOOSING MATERIALS AND CHEMICALS: IMPLICATIONS FOR SUSTAINABLE PRODUCT DESIGN

Adopting a precautionary approach to using chemicals and choosing materials can be a significant step in the transition toward creating sustainable products and services. Materials selection is relevant to all five sustainable product design criteria as it influences worker safety, consumer and environmental health, community benefits, and economic viability.

A recent report by Clean Production Action describes a four-phase journey for businesses in relation to their use of toxic chemicals (Greiner, Rossi, Thorpe, & Kerr, 2006). In phase one, a company denies that hazards exist. In phase two, the company is aware of hazards and strives toward environmental compliance. In phase three, the company has moved beyond compliance to target high-hazard chemicals, and in phase four, the company is actively researching "green" chemicals and materials.

In light of this framework, the Q'ewar Project, though not a corporate entity, is clearly a phase four organization, as the project directors are actively seeking to make their products safe and healthy for workers, the earth, and consumers. They choose local, natural materials and are making an effort to transition fully from synthetic chemicals to plant-based dyes. The Käthe Kruse doll company falls somewhere between phases two and three. It certainly strives to comply with all regulations and therefore tests for phthalates and other chemicals that are restricted under European law. It is not actively looking for alternatives to toxic chemicals that are an important part of its production process, such as polystyrene and PVC, but it does prioritize the purchase of Öko-Tex labeled textiles which form the bulk of its input materials. The American Girl company also appears to fall between phases two and three. The company strives for environmental compliance and is working to increase energy efficiency and make its packaging more environmentally friendly. It complies with the EU directive on phthalates, but is not leading the way by actively seeking alternatives to toxic chemicals.

Another issue is locating suppliers that offer materials that enhance sustainability. The Q'ewar Project, for example, tries to obtain all its materials locally, including alpaca, wool, and cotton; doing so benefits local farmers. Only a few materials such as thread and fasteners are purchased from distant locations, as they are not produced locally. The project contributes to the local economy by purchasing materials locally and hiring local people to process materials such as alpaca fiber and to make the dolls and doll clothing.

The Käthe Kruse doll company obtains its materials from a much wider range of sources than the Q'ewar Project, including Chinese suppliers for some doll parts and doll clothing and Indian suppliers for human hair for doll wigs. It purchases the bulk of materials and chemicals within Europe, including reindeer hair from Scandinavia, textiles from Austria, Spain, and Switzerland, and chemicals from Germany. A large multinational corporation such as Mattel has an extremely globalized supply chain. Daniel Cohen (2005) has described the supply chain for the Barbie doll as including molds from the United States, plastic and hair from Taiwan and Japan, and assembly in the Philippines or in other lower wage locations such as Indonesia or China. When materials are transported around the globe to support production in low-wage countries and then the finished product is transported to buyers in industrialized countries, there are significant environmental impacts from energy and materials use.

TRANSPARENCY AND SUSTAINABILITY

The Internet has led to changes in information technologies that make it easier for toy companies to subcontract their production around the world. It has also made it harder for multinational corporations to control the flow of information about what goes on behind factory walls. In 2001 at a meeting of the World Economic Forum, the CEO of Hasbro, Alan Hassenfeld, noted "the fact is that the Internet makes us totally open-there is nowhere for the corporation to hide" (Vogl, 2001, p. 2).

But the corporate toy world is not truly transparent. The industry works to control the information that is released and is not forthcoming about working conditions or hazardous chemicals used in production. Not surprisingly, it prefers self-regulation over government intervention. As described in chapter 2, the International Council of Toy Industries (ICTI), an international association of toy trade organizations, adopted a code of conduct in 1995, under pressure from advocacy groups and trade unions. ICTI encourages member companies to adhere to this code of conduct and has developed the CARE monitoring process, which allows a factory to be certified as being in compliance with the Code of Business Practices. ICTI has identified accredited audit firms to be used in the certification process and maintains a database of certified factories on its Web site.[5]

A weakness of the ICTI CARE process is that it does not involve outside stakeholders such as human rights advocacy groups, governments, or consumers,

[5] See http://www.toy-icti.org

so its credibility is limited. It serves the toy industry well: manufacturers can now assure their customers that they are complying with this code. For example, employees at Käthe Kruse told me they received ICTI certification from the factories with whom they contracted in China. However, it is not a stretch of the imagination to wonder whether the ICTI certification process is simply a paper exercise. Unless the process and results are fully transparent, the certification has limited value. Advocacy organizations, such as Swedwatch based in Sweden, have called for increased access to information from ICTI such as audit summaries (Bjurling, 2004).

Mattel prides itself on being the only toy company that is not only monitoring its factories and having an independent organization conduct verification audits, but is also making the audit reports publicly available. As it notes on its Web site, "we publicly disclose these independent monitoring reports for the world to see—both our successes and challenges. We are the only toy company, and one of the few in the consumer products industry, to do this."[6]

However, as part of its agreement with the International Center on Corporate Accountability (ICCA), Mattel has the opportunity to review draft audit reports and to correct mistakes before reports are made public. If ICCA and Mattel disagree, the report is still made available to the public, with Mattel's comments included in a separate document.

Still, Mattel's "transparency" is very controlled. The Asia Monitor Resource Center (AMRC) notes that Mattel does not share the details of the standards behind its Global Manufacturing Principles (GMP) or its audit tools or procedures, so it is difficult to review the reports and understand exactly what was audited. The AMRC has called for greater transparency and full disclosure of audit tools to increase public trust in these reports (Wong & Frost, 2000). The AMRC also notes that there are no surprise visits. Factory managers have advance notice and can spruce up the factory and prepare employees as needed.

Activist organizations such as the AMRC are calling for companies to involve workers in developing and implementing the GMP. The Fair Trade Center and SwedWatch, two advocacy organizations based in Sweden, published a report that concluded that workers must be involved in implementing and enforcing codes of conduct (Bjurling, 2004). Workers are most familiar with day-to-day plant conditions and could provide valuable information if they were fully involved in the auditing process. However, many workers still do not know of these standards. The ICCA's 2007 audit of Mattel's Chinese vendor plants found that between 30% and 52% of workers were unfamiliar with the standards (ICCA, 2008). Although a sample of workers is interviewed during the audit process, workers' voices do not appear in the reports and they may not be able to participate honestly in the auditing process.

[6]See http://www.mattel.com

Until workers understand the requirements of the GMP and are able to openly participate without fear of punishment by their employer, they cannot fully engage in its implementation.

Some corporations in other industry sectors have begun to acknowledge the limitations of codes of conduct and traditional inspections. Levi Strauss, for example, found that during 10 years of inspections, inaccurate information was often provided. The company now involves workers in regular meetings with plant management to follow up on its code of conduct. This provides workers with a real opportunity to exert some influence and improve conditions (Bjurling, 2004).

Human rights advocates also recommend that companies work closely with trade unions to support workers' rights (Bjurling, 2004). In general, workers in China have little voice, as freedom of association is restricted and independent trade unions are not allowed. The All China Federation of Trade Unions (ACFTU) is the only trade union allowed in China, with 120 million members. This union is not independent; it is run by the Chinese government and has close ties to the Communist Party. In July 2007 the Chinese government passed a comprehensive labor law that took effect in January 2008. This legislation requires that contracts be in writing and that workers be informed of job requirements, conditions, and compensation. This legislation, opposed by many multinational corporations, was weakened from its original form. The ACFTU is responsible for overseeing the implementation of these new regulations and some question whether this law will be strongly enforced (Barboza, 2006; Blanchette, 2007).

It is not unusual for a multinational corporation to want to control the flow of information. Although Mattel touts its transparency, the company management of both American Girl and Mattel declined to participate in this study.[7] The transparency offered by posting reports and sharing public relations materials on the web is quite limited and does not truly reveal the company's practices. In contrast, at my field research site in Germany everyone affiliated with the Käthe Kruse doll company made a genuine effort to provide me with information I requested during my visit and in follow-up discussions via e-mail. My initial contacts with the Q'ewar Project in Peru were two American women (one based in Vermont and one in Cusco) who are active supporters of the initiative and serve as gatekeepers for the project. Once they understood my research intentions I was welcomed into the community that is the Q'ewar Project. These experiences of true transparency gave me the confidence that these organizations were not hiding crucial information.

---

[7]American Girl informed me that they get so many requests from students that they did not have time to participate. More importantly they noted that "our doll design and production methods are proprietary and not something we disclose to the public."

ECONOMIC CHALLENGES TO SUSTAINABILITY

There are significant economic challenges to sustainability as a strategic vision and strategy. For example, consider economic viability, one of the five elements of the sustainable product design framework I outlined in chapter 3. One criterion is that the product be priced for economic viability and also that costs be internalized to enable production that is environmentally sound and socially just. This goal is at odds with our current economic system, which rewards companies that are able to effectively externalize these costs. As discussed below, the three cases described in this study face different types of economic challenges due to their location and the scale on which they operate.

Although the Q'ewar Project and the Käthe Kruse doll company both have the intention to utilize high-quality, environmentally friendly materials, their actual purchasing experience illustrates the different range of choices available to an enterprise located in a wealthy industrialized country versus one located in an impoverished, developing country. Because the Öko-Tex labeling program is well recognized in Europe, purchasers for Käthe Kruse have a wide range of color, design, and fiber choices when choosing eco-friendly textiles. In contrast, although the Q'ewar project directors would like to produce a 100% organic product, they have had difficulty finding a supplier of organic cotton. A few cotton producers in Peru have begun producing organic cotton but the product is primarily exported to Europe, where organic fibers can command a high price. The domestic textile market in Peru consists mostly of inexpensive, affordable synthetic fibers, so the Q'ewar Project has very limited choices when procuring cotton textiles to make its doll "skins" and some doll clothing.

As noted earlier the global toy market is intensely competitive and companies must continually innovate to survive. That the Käthe Kruse doll company celebrated its 100th anniversary in 2005 is a testament to its ability to innovate and to continue to provide a quality product. The company's disparate strategies for developing new markets in the last 15 years point out the challenges of implementing a sustainability vision. Käthe Kruse has been quite successful in developing its Waldorf line of toys for a European and North American market. A number of these toys have received certification from the German Waldorf Association, which indicates they are made of natural materials. The company did not want to be limited to this market only and considered other factors in the product design such as functionality. For example, some of the Waldorf-style baby toys are stuffed with polypropylene pellets rather than wool, which make them more easily washable. The company also has introduced several new lines of vinyl dolls for young and preteen children as a way to compete with similar dolls on the market. These design decisions have been based on the economics of the toy market rather than a precautionary approach to chemical use.

Even though the Q'ewar Project is not designed as a profit-making enterprise, it must meet consumer requirements and have an ongoing market to survive economically. The dolls, as initially designed, were clothed in dress that was indigenous to several villages in the Andes. However, the project directors quickly discovered that the market for dolls in such dress was limited. Adults bought one or two dolls in "village" dress and the market was quickly saturated. Children wanted dolls in modern clothes that they could put on and take off easily. Therefore the designers altered some of the clothing designs to reflect these preferences. By using local materials such as alpaca the project has maintained a Peruvian identity and look for the dolls. The directors have also introduced smaller dolls, which have proven to be very popular, as they are a good size for child play and are less expensive than the large dolls.

American Girl/Mattel faces a different set of economic challenges as it operates on an extremely large scale, with many factories employing over 5,000 workers. Because the industry is extremely competitive, companies are driven to cut costs wherever possible. Although Mattel is leading the way in attempting to improve working conditions by implementing its Global Manufacturing Principles, change comes very slowly. Mattel spends approximately $10 million annually on monitoring but many activists believe that the company does not do enough to share the costs of its ethical demands with its vendors (Goldman, 2004). Suppliers are under great pressure to produce toys at low costs with short delivery times. Providing humane working conditions entails costs in terms of wages, and improvements in infrastructure, training, and equipment. Until the toy industry shares more of these costs with its suppliers it is likely that false information will continue to be reported in factory inspections (Bjurling, 2004).

In this chapter, I have attempted to articulate cross-cutting themes that are relevant in a journey toward sustainable product design, production, and consumption. First and foremost, there must be a vision and an intention toward sustainability. From this flows a precautionary approach to chemicals and materials use, a work environment that is designed for human dignity, and transparent communication about the product and the production process, as there is nothing to hide when this vision and intention is driving decision making. In addition, designing a work environment so that a product can be made with care has implications for worker health and safety and consumer health and satisfaction with the product. Also, scale matters when designing a work environment for sustainability. Large-scale enterprises like Mattel face different challenges than small initiatives like the Q'ewar Project that can readily attend to the needs of individual employees. In addition, our economic system poses many challenges to implementing a sustainability vision as the true costs of production and consumption are externalized. In the next chapter, I reflect more broadly on the concept of a sustainable product, its connection to sustainable production and consumption, and the changes that are needed to actualize this vision.

CHAPTER 8

Paradigm Shifting or Incremental Change? Some Thoughts on Sustainable Product Design, Production, and Consumption

The *American Heritage Dictionary* defines a product as "anything produced by human or mechanical effort or by a natural process" (Morris, 1969). Products are material objects that serve a function in society. This function may be associated with the necessities of daily life such as food, shelter, clothing, or transportation or it may be purely for recreation or pleasure or other uses. As a society, we produce, consume, and dispose of millions of products daily. At the point of purchase, the consumer rarely evaluates what it took to make the product from the perspective of materials, energy, and human labor or what happens at its "end of life." Rather, the average customer considers price, functionality, aesthetics, and quality.

In conceptualizing a **sustainable** product, I attempted to go behind the façade of the finished product to better understand the environmental, social, and economic aspects of design, production, and consumption. In the current model of globalization, in which most production occurs at a great distance from the point of consumption, this embedded history is not obvious to most consumers. Nor do many producers account for it, as they externalize the environmental and social costs of production. Some researchers have studied the embedded energy of products and analyzed material flows as part of a product life-cycle analysis. My purpose is not to quantify the use of energy or materials, but to consider these issues more qualitatively. That is, what is the significance of design choices? What do they imply for workers, communities, and the environment throughout the supply chain—and for consumers of that product?

By connecting the term "sustainable" to "product," we add many layers of meaning, and thus raise expectations for a radically different approach to design, production, and consumption. Sustainable product design calls for fundamentally new thinking that is not compartmentalized. It builds on the eco design principles of detoxification and dematerialization. That is, it calls for alternatives to materials that are toxic, persistent, bioaccumulative, or scarce, and requires that material and energy usage be reduced significantly. Alternatives assessment[1] of chemicals and materials is a growing field, as is the development of green chemistry[2] and bio-based materials. In addition, product-service systems are increasingly being developed to help reduce materials use. But sustainable product design goes beyond eco design to include "humanization," which encompasses the social impacts of production and consumption, including a range of factors described in chapter 3 (MacPherson, 2004).

The design elements of humanization get at the deeper purpose of products, production, and consumption in our society. After all, what is the purpose of a product? The case studies in this book reveal very different intentions. The Q'ewar doll is being produced to help create sustainable livelihoods for the impoverished young women of Andahuaylillas, Peru. The vision of the project is personal empowerment and community development. Designing a work environment that is supportive and encourages these women to find their voices is more important than the material object that is being produced. However, the product is also designed with care to engage young children with an object that is pleasing and developmentally appropriate. The finished doll enters the marketplace as a commodity to be sold and provides economic resources that are necessary to "grow" the project, but the commercial element is secondary to the broader intent. The true product here is sustainable livelihoods.

For the Käthe Kruse doll company, the intention is to provide a toy that meets the needs of children and is also safe, soft, and realistic. As a corporate entity, Käthe Kruse's products enter the marketplace to generate profits for the company. The original intention of the Pleasant company, which created the American Girl doll, was to teach history to girls through books and an accompanying material object, a doll. This intent was realized through the creation of 13 historical dolls. The company has gone far beyond this original intention to its current metamorphosis into a company that "celebrates girlhood" through its many books, dolls, and accessories, and at the same time encourages preteens to become consumers.

Two of these cases represent corporate models that are primarily attentive to the economic bottom line, rather than to the triple bottom line described in chapter 7. Yet even among these two corporate models we find different purposes and different choices in design, production, and consumption. In contrast,

---

[1] Alternatives assessment is a newly emerging framework and set of methodologies to compare a toxic chemical in use with possible alternatives, to find a substitute that is safer for workers, consumers, and ecosystems (Rossi, Tickner, & Geiser, 2006).

[2] Green chemistry is a scientific approach to reduce or eliminate hazardous chemicals and waste by designing environmentally friendly processes and chemicals. Anastas and Warner (1998) have delineated 12 principles for green chemistry.

the Q'ewar Project represents an enterprise in which the product is in the service of the worker rather than the other way around. It is worth a moment to carefully contemplate this model, rather than dismiss it as unrealistic on a broader scale, as it can provide a vision for radical change.

Imagine if the first intention of design, production, and consumption was to create products and production systems that truly benefited workers, communities, and consumers and had minimal impacts on the earth. Then our society would truly be moving toward a "restorative" economy, described by Paul Hawken (1993) as one that eliminates waste from industrial production, makes resource use cyclical rather than linear, shifts to a solar and hydrogen-based economy, and creates systems of feedback and accountability that support restorative behavior (p. 209). Imagine if businesses created products for human development and empowerment rather than primarily for economic profit and if the prices of products reflected the true costs of production and consumption. These two changes would put our society on a solid path toward sustainability. These changes would reflect a paradigm shift in product design, production, and consumption, something we cannot accomplish by tinkering at the edges of current business systems and models.

It is in striving to meet the humanization criteria that we need the most radical change in design. Despite the difficulty of implementing "design for environment," it is easier to accomplish than ensuring humane working conditions. Yet all these changes are needed to fully meet the definition of a sustainable product. In "design for environment" the challenge is to reduce the use of materials, energy, and toxins, without a resulting rebound effect where consumption increases and negates the environmental benefit of the design. Efforts toward safer materials choices and energy efficiency that do not help humanize the work itself accomplish incremental change but are not transformational.

To design for the humanizing of work, we will have to rethink our relationships with machines, and reconsider the trade-offs between focusing on efficiency versus developing human potential and human dignity. We must also seek ways to democratize the workplace and engage workers in decision making about the production process. The Q'ewar Project and the Käthe Kruse doll company provide glimpses of the potential to humanize the work environment through care, intention, and design for human dignity and to enhance the value of the product itself by making it with care.

I now turn to a discussion of scale, linkages with systems of sustainable production and consumption, and the roles of different actors in these systems.

THE CHALLENGES OF SCALE

The Käthe Kruse doll company and the Q'ewar Project represent small-scale enterprises whose managers can address the needs of individuals and the details of craft production. In the dominant model of toy production, where thousands of workers are laboring 12 to 18 hours a day in huge factories to produce products on an assembly line, it is much more difficult to implement sustainable product design. Theoretically, management could develop a comprehensive chemicals policy and work to eliminate toxic, persistent, and bioaccumulative chemicals in the production process. Management could increase energy and materials efficiency and reduce waste by implementing production process changes. These incremental changes can occur within the existing work environment and existing systems of control and power.

It is much more difficult to accomplish the humanization aspect of sustainable product design by making incremental changes. Mattel's implementation of the Global Manufacturing Principles is one example of an attempt to make incremental improvements through controlling work hours and ensuring that people are paid and receive the benefits to which they are entitled. But these changes have not accomplished much in the direction of truly humanizing the workplace in these toy factories. To create a truly humane work environment would require radical change. For example, beyond cutting work hours, raising wages, and improving dormitory conditions, it would mean redesigning factories to make better use of human potential and training workers to take on increasing responsibility. It would mean involving workers in decision making about the production process. It would also mean designing a work environment that was truly "family-friendly," with facilities such as high quality on-site childcare and living accommodations for families. It might also mean redesigning work so that some aspects of it could be done safely in small factories in the workers' home communities, as a way to keep families intact and reduce rural to urban migration.

One interesting alternative to migration to export processing zones is being demonstrated in the Andean villages of Huanta and Huamanga in Peru.[3] In 2006 the Converse shoe company began shipping shoes from a factory in Vietnam to these villages, where skilled embroiderers add decorative designs. This project is financed by a Belgian development agency in cooperation with the Peruvian Ministry of Women and Social Development. Over 13,000 women are now benefiting from this project, which draws on the traditional skills and knowledge of these women, who are expert weavers and embroiderers. The International Labor Organization (2006) calls this an example of "the bright face of globalization" (para. 12). Although the company holds to high quality standards and strict production deadlines, women work in community with one another to get their job done. Rather than leave their villages and families to find employment, they can continue to weave and embroider in their own communities. As in the Q'ewar Project, the workers receive counseling and support if they are victims

---

[3] In the 1980s, the residents of this region of Peru suffered greatly from violence associated with the Shining Path, a Maoist guerilla organization in Peru. The residents are very impoverished and few jobs exist in this rural economy.

of domestic violence and the project directors are hoping to build self-esteem in these women by having them work in community with others. Unlike the Q'ewar Project, however, this project has engaged a multinational corporation to make use of human capital and traditional skills and knowledge.

Another aspect of scale must also be considered. Large-scale factories such as those described in this book meet consumer demand by churning out extremely large numbers of dolls. Craft production as described in the Q'ewar Project and Käthe Kruse case studies simply cannot produce enough dolls to meet consumer desires worldwide. This makes it all the more critical to redesign large-scale facilities so they can be humane work environments.

LINKING SUSTAINABLE PRODUCT DESIGN, PRODUCTION, AND CONSUMPTION

As described in chapter 3, sustainable product design is intimately linked with systems of sustainable production and consumption. Before sustainable product design can be fully implemented, systems must be in place that support sustainable production and consumption. These include government, corporate, and citizen-based strategies such as regulations to phase out toxic chemicals, economic incentives for sustainable product development, institutional purchasing policies that specify a preference for sustainable products, detailed product labeling, transparent and effective codes of conduct and standards, and increased public pressure for humane working conditions, as well as comprehensive environmental management. Figure 1, also in chapter 3, p. 43 as Figure 4, indicates how these design elements interact with systems of sustainable production and consumption. In the rest of this chapter I describe the roles that different actors must play. The production of toys—or any consumer good—will not become truly sustainable without the participation of designers, governments, citizens, and corporations.

Stuart Walker (2006), a leading industrial design thinker, describes the factors that contribute to products becoming obsolescent, including disposability, wear, non-repairability, and functional, technological, and aesthetic obsolescence. He notes that while the useful life of most products is short, they are designed with "permanent" materials; he argues that designers must develop a new design approach that acknowledges the short lives of products and designs them accordingly. Although most would say that fashion or fads mediate against sustainability, Walker argues that designers must also understand that fashion is also about creativity and new solutions, which could be harnessed toward more sustainable practices. He believes that rather than designing for product longevity, we must all acknowledge that products designed for today may not be appropriate for the future. Therefore these fashionable objects should be designed in a way that places the smallest burden on the earth and also provides a healthy work environment.

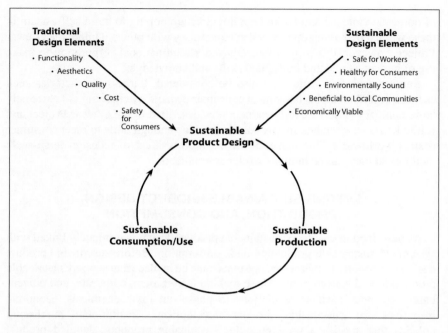

Figure 1. Linking sustainable product design, sustainable production, and sustainable consumption.

In contrast, designer Jonathan Chapman (2005) argues for a new relationship with objects that he terms "emotionally durable design." He sees the wasting of objects as a symptom of "expired empathy" and argues for designs that increase the lifespan of this emotion. Rather than considering durability only from the physical perspective, Chapman believes designers need to consider the human desire for products and other factors that influence the duration of empathy or connection that we have with the objects around us.

These concepts present significant challenges to industrial designers who are not currently taught to frame design questions like these or to choose materials that address these issues of sustainability. On the one hand, designers must strive to create products that are durable and long-lasting; on the other, they must acknowledge that designs may have a short lifespan, and use materials that are appropriate for this duration. Design schools have not traditionally wrestled with these concepts, though some institutions are beginning to incorporate them.

The road toward sustainable production and consumption starts with the design process, but design cannot be left to the industrial designer only. Design must include everyone who has a design-making role throughout the supply chain—including the industrial designer, engineer, production worker, middle manager, and CEO. A company that has committed to a sustainability agenda must integrate the product design process as it maps out its strategic direction, and ensure that the design process incorporates the concepts of detoxification, dematerialization, and humanization.

The parameters of sustainable product design provide many opportunities for innovation. Yet this innovation is unlikely to occur on a large scale unless governments support market and regulatory drivers that encourage firms to develop eco-friendly products. Governments can support such progress in many ways. They can offer incentives to develop safer materials and renewable energy. They can ban or phase out toxic chemicals. They can eliminate subsidies for fossil fuels and mining. They can create labeling programs and purchasing policies that prefer these products. Stronger support is needed for green chemistry approaches that develop substances that are "benign by design." In the absence of leadership from the federal government, states are taking the lead in this area. In addition, organizations such as the Green Chemistry and Commerce Council are promoting research and practice in green chemistry and engineering across industry sectors.[4]

How do we insure that products are safe and healthy for consumers? A first step is for businesses to have the intention, and a strategy, that prioritizes consumer health and safety. This value must be communicated to product designers so they are encouraged to choose the safest materials and chemicals in production. It also requires that systems are in place to ensure the integrity of the design throughout the supply chain until it reaches consumers. This will require significant policy change at the level of the federal government, including revamping of federal product safety laws to increase the regulatory authority of the U.S. Consumer Products Safety Commission.[5] It will also require an overhaul of the federal chemicals management law, the Toxics Substances Control Act (TSCA). This law, passed in 1976, grandfathered in all chemicals on the market at the time and required the U.S. EPA to prove that a chemical was harmful before it could be restricted. Very few chemicals have been restricted under the act. Instead, thousands of chemicals are currently in use that have not been adequately tested for safety. Many policy makers and activists are now calling for new legislation along the lines of the European Union's new REACH program (Registration, Evaluation, Authorisation and Restriction of Chemicals) that requires chemical manufacturers to register the chemicals they produce and to provide basic toxicity information.

---

[4]The mission of the Green Chemistry and Commerce Council is to promote and support green chemistry and the design for environment approach to research and practices nationally and internationally among companies and other governmental and nongovernmental entities. See http://greenchemistryandcommerce.org/greenchemistry.php

[5]The Consumer Product Safety Improvement Act (CPSIA), signed into law in August 2008, makes some of these needed changes.

The toy industry is beginning to recognize the need for improvement in ensuring product safety. For example, in light of recent toy recalls, the industry is working with the American National Standards Institute to develop a conformity assessment system to ensure compliance with safety standards throughout the supply chain (Bhatia, 2007). This system includes third-party auditing and certification (Toy Safety Coordination Initiative, 2008). Conformity assessment, if properly implemented, will ensure that toys are in compliance with current safety standards. However, this process does not ensure toy safety, as the standards require testing for only a limited number of hazardous chemicals that may be used in toy production. For example, the current regulations require testing for only eight heavy metals and the six phthalates recently banned by the CPSIA. The industry opposed legislation signed into law in the State of Washington in April 2008 that will require toy manufacturers to disclose chemicals of high concern that are in children's products.

Consumers vote with their purchases. If the "psychological distance" between production and consumption is shortened, consumers will understand the embedded environmental and social history of the products they buy (Princen, 2002). As independent third-party labeling makes more information available on the sustainability of products, institutional and individual consumers will be able to influence the marketplace through their purchasing decisions. Providing this information is an important role for activists, especially with regard to the toy industry, where enchantment is "branded" and an increased awareness of the hazards of toy making could impact consumer choices (Langer, 2004). Even if sweatshops cannot be eliminated, activists must be vigilant in exposing them. As citizens of the world, we cannot accept the mythology that as long as the economy is booming overall, hazards to individual workers are acceptable. These workers, often poor, uneducated, young women, cannot be another throwaway product of industrialization.

A label indicating that a toy is "fair-trade" or "sustainable," building on the model of fair-trade coffee and chocolate, would provide information for consumers to differentiate between toys on the basis of how they are made. In addition, an annual list of "sustainably designed toys" could provide a positive counterpoint to lists of dangerous and inappropriate toys that circulate during the December holidays. Figure 2 provides examples of programs that increase transparency about how products are made. The challenge here is to avoid overwhelming consumers with too much information; still, most purchasers care about more than one attribute, and an integrated score would provide useful information.

One of the greatest challenges for corporations engaged in a journey toward corporate social responsibility is to determine how to design integrated solutions. Humans are skilled at identifying problems and then dividing them up into manageable pieces in order to address them. Unfortunately, this approach often results in compartmentalized solutions that do not get at root causes. The toy recalls of the summer of 2007 provide a cautionary tale in this regard. Mattel, an

*The **Fair Trade Certified** label certifies that farmers receive fair prices for their products and that working conditions are humane. In addition, sustainable agriculture and community development are supported, as fair trade revenues are invested in local projects. http://www.transfairusa.org/

*The **Forest Stewardship Council** is focused on responsible management of forests around the world. The organization has developed 10 principles and 57 criteria that address legal issues, indigenous rights, labor rights, multiple benefits, and environmental impacts surrounding forest management. http://www.fscus.org/

***EcoLogo** provides third-party certification of environmentally preferred products in over 120 product and service categories. http://www.ecologo.org

***Green Seal** promotes environmentally sound products by providing third-party certification for a range of products, including cleaning products, windows, paper, and paints. http://www.greenseal.org/

***Healthytoys.org** has tested over 1500 toys and children's products for cadmium, lead, bromine, arsenic, chlorine, and mercury. The site provides a ranking of toys, information about toxic chemicals that may be in children's products, and ideas for taking action to ensure that children's products are safer and healthier. http://www.healthytoys.org

***GoodGuide.com** is a new site that provides information on the health, environmental, and social performance of products and companies. As of April 2009, the site included information on 70,000 foods, toys, personal care, and household products. Consumers can focus on a particular attribute of concern or use the integrated score to choose preferred products. http://www.goodguide.com

Figure 2. Examples of programs that increase transparency about the environmental and social costs of products throughout their life cycles.

industry leader in addressing the problem of working conditions in toy factories in China, was seemingly caught by surprise when its Global Manufacturing Principles did not prevent millions of its toys from being recalled for high lead paint levels and design flaws, including tiny magnets that could come loose and be ingested, posing an intestinal hazard. A former board member of the ICCA, Murray Weidenbaum, told the *New York Times* that, in retrospect, the GMP mission was narrower than it should have been. Said Weidenbaum, "We focused on the working conditions, because that was our task, and because the critics at the time were focusing on it—child labor, prison labor, all that. It turns out we missed the big picture, which is the nature of the product" (Dee, 2007, p. 5). The entire production process, including materials and chemical choices, and the design of the work itself, must be integrated in creating sustainable production and consumption systems.

Multinational corporations must recognize a broader view of social responsibility that goes beyond making short-term profits for their shareholders. Redesigning products according to eco design principles can be an important first step for corporations that are operating in countries where health, safety, and environmental laws are not enforced. The elimination of known toxic chemicals in the production process may do more to protect workers than the attempt to ensure worker safety and proper environmental management of hazardous chemicals through codes of conduct. These codes are a step in the right direction, but they have proven very difficult to implement.

At the same time, of course, products must be responsive to market requirements and must be profitable to the firm. Often, the implementation of pollution prevention practices and eco design results in increased production efficiency, which can reduce costs and increase profits. Also, eliminating toxic chemicals from the production process avoids the costs and liabilities associated with waste management. Good corporate citizenship practices can also help improve the economic viability of a firm because they create trust with key stakeholders.

Many companies, especially those that operate internationally, understand that as their markets expand in developing countries, they must contribute positively to the social and economic development of the communities where production occurs. The Boston College Center for Corporate Citizenship (2006) has developed a framework to describe the importance of community engagement that addresses local social challenges and goes beyond providing jobs and paying taxes.[6] Many companies are beginning to make these community investments. Examples are extremely varied, such as teaching rural women in India to start micro enterprises or offering free community medical care (Engardio, 2007). Innovest Strategic Partners, a socially responsible investment firm, has identified the 100 most sustainable firms in the world.[7] Although the methodology is imperfect, it demonstrates that investors increasingly understand that social and environmental performance is relevant to financial performance and that they are looking for evidence of these commitments.

A truly sustainable product does not exist today, nor do sustainable systems of production and consumption. However, many companies are striving to improve the sustainability of their products, and government policy makers and activists are working to create the conditions that support these efforts. The framework in this book, by presenting five key elements of sustainable product design, offers a new pathway. This framework can be engaged at any point and utilized as a

[6] See http://www.bcccc.net
[7] See http://www.global100.org

compass for the future as well as a continuum for the present, with many opportunities for improvement. Some companies will focus on eliminating toxic inputs from production, while others will focus on improving working conditions and providing community benefits. These small, practical steps are vital in moving toward a society where consumers expect sustainable products and producers routinely provide them.

We need both incremental change and a paradigm shift—a revolution in thinking, awareness, and action—to progress on the path toward sustainable product design and ultimately the broader goal of a sustainable society. We must be able to visualize and work toward the larger framework of transformational change while implementing these smaller steps. Often incremental change is more practical and more palatable to individuals and organizations that are resistant to a disruption in business as usual. However, to move beyond incremental change a broader vision is needed as a compass to guide our intentions and actions. Sustainable product design criteria can serve as such a compass by offering a vision that values safe and healthy workers, consumers, communities, ecosystems and economies, rather than a view that assumes that trade-offs are necessary in the name of progress.

APPENDIX

Evaluation of Sustainable Design Elements for Each Case Study

Table 1. Summary of Sustainable Design Elements for the American Girl Doll

Sustainable Product Design Elements	Meets criteria in full	Meets criteria in part	Does not meet criteria	Additional information needed to evaluate
SAFE for workers		Mattel is enforcing rules against child labor. Conditions at American Girl headquarters, distribution centers, and retail stores are likely to meet criteria.	Employees in production facilities work long hours at low wages; hours and pace may be excessive. Employees do not have adequate health and safety training or PPE. Chemicals used in production present hazards to workers. Some dormitory conditions are unsatisfactory. Workers do not have freedom of association. Workers do not have job control or input into production process. Workers in industrial cotton and textile production face chemical and other hazards.	Did not visit factories in China or American Girl corporate headquarters in Wisconsin, so data are from reports by NGOs and ICCA (nonprofit organization that audits Mattel-owned and vendor factories.)
HEALTHY for consumers	Dolls are developmentally appropriate. Dolls meet EU and U.S. safety standards.			

ENVIRONMENTALLY sound	Dolls are durable, repairable, and can be disassembled—doll hospital is important product-service system. Plastic waste is reused in injection molding. Some petroleum-based solvents have been replaced by water-based solvents. Some packaging is environmentally preferable.	Chemicals used in vinyl production are environmental hazards. Industrial cotton and wool production is hazardous to the environment. Industrial wool production uses hazardous chemicals. Plastic dolls are not recyclable. Millions of catalogs are distributed annually.	Additional data are needed to determine energy and materials efficiency of factories. Do not have data on whether water-based solvents are being substituted widely or in only a few instances.
BENEFICIAL to local communities	Financial donations from the American Girl Company and Pleasant Rowland have greatly benefited the Madison arts community, environmental education efforts, and other nonprofit organizations in the United States.	Profits from doll sales have not directly benefited the communities in which the dolls are made.	Do not have data on benefits that may accrue to Chinese communities where factories located, but it appears that benefit is to the overall economy and not to individual workers or local community.
ECONOMICALLY viable	Sales have risen over 20 years in contrast to declining Barbie sales.	Environmental and social costs of production are externalized.	Detailed data on revenues/ sales/costs of production are not available.

Table 2. Summary of Sustainable Design Elements for the Käthe Kruse Doll

Sustainable Product Design Elements	Meets criteria in full	Meets criteria in part	Does not meet criteria	Additional information needed to evaluate
SAFE for workers		Workplace is clean, well lit. Workers have some control over daily activities. Craft production—pace and hours are not excessive. Workers receive health and safety training.	Chemicals used in polyurethane, polystyrene, and vinyl production present hazards to workers. Workers in industrial cotton production face chemical and other hazards; sourcing of organic cotton will reduce these hazards.	Exposure to toxic chemicals was not measured. Did not observe working conditions in Latvia or China.
HEALTHY for consumers	Dolls are developmentally appropriate. Dolls meet EU and U.S. safety standards. Cloth dolls use high quality Öko-Tex certified textiles, which are safe for the consumer.			Plastic dolls are tested for nonylphenols and phthalates—may be difficult to ensure that all dolls are free of these chemicals.

ENVIRONMENTALLY sound	Cloth dolls use Öko-Tex 100 certified textiles. Dolls are durable, repairable, and can be disassembled. Materials diversity is minimized, renewable resources used. Waste is minimized.	Chemicals used in polyurethane, polystyrene, and vinyl production are hazardous to the environment. Industrial cotton production is hazardous to the environment; sourcing of organic cotton will reduce this hazard. Wool production uses hazardous chemicals. Plastic dolls are not recyclable.	Öko-Tex 100 certified textiles are not necessarily produced in an environmentally sound way, but some factories have Öko-Tex 1000 certification to indicate eco-friendly production practices. Additional data needed to determine energy efficiency of factory.
BENEFICIAL to local communities	Company has longevity in community—60 years. Supportive to family life—Flexible work hours, ability to leave company and return part-time.		Wages are average for textile industry—additional data needed to determine if living wage.
ECONOMICALLY viable	Company in existence for 100 years, in Donauwörth for 60 years. Recent diversification of product lines to stay competitive. Low worker turnover and high satisfaction with work environment.	Environmental and social costs are not fully internalized.	

Table 3. Summary of Sustainable Product Elements for the Q'ewar Project Doll

Sustainable Product Design Elements	Meets criteria in full	Meets criteria in part	Does not meet criteria	Additional information needed to evaluate
SAFE for workers		The Q'ewar Project work environment is safe for workers. Health hazards are minimal.	Aniline dyes are used in the making of doll ponchos and shawls—this occurs off-site and is being phased out.	Unable to observe work environment for fiber and textile production so cannot evaluate safety of entire supply chain.
HEALTHY for consumers	This product is healthy for consumers—is development-ally appropriate, soft, safe, made of natural materials.			
ENVIRON-MENTALLY sound		Natural, renewable materials are used and production is on a small scale so that materials are not used at rate greater than regenerative capacity.	Aniline dyes used in one aspect of produc-tion process—goal is to eliminate in favor of plant dyes.	
BENEFICIAL to local communities	Project is designed to empower community and is providing a sustainable liveli-hood. Profits are reinvested in community. Work design promotes community input and participation.			
ECONOMICALLY viable		Project is stable in its philosophy. Profits are reinvested. Employees are well utilized. Communication is valued.		Difficult to know if product will be economically viable in the long-term because of limited market for this doll. Unclear whether innovation will be sufficient to meet market requirements.

References

Acosta-Alzuru, C., & Roushanzamir, E. P. (2003). Everything we do is a celebration of you!: Pleasant Company constructs American girlhood. *The Communication Review, 6,* 45-69.

American Girl Company Press Release. (2005, August 22). Retrieved June 12, 2006, from http://www.americangirl.com/corp/media/2005/0822ican.html

American Girl Company Press Release. (2005, December 26). Retrieved June 12, 2006, from http://www.americangirl.com/corp/media/2005/1226girlsinc.html

Anastas, P., & Warner, J. (1998). *Green chemistry: Theory and practice.* New York: Oxford University Press.

Arndorfer, J. B. (2005, December 12). American Girl campaign offers to save childhood. *Advertising Age.* Retrieved June 15, 2006, from http://www.adage.com

Auer, P., Besse, G., & Méda, D. (Eds.). (2005). *Offshoring and the internationalization of employment—A challenge for a fair globalization?* In Proceedings of the International Labour Organization Symposium, Annecy, France, 1-16.

Babich, M. (1998). *The risk of chronic toxicity associated with exposure to diisononyl phthalate (DINP) in children's products.* Bethesda, MD: U.S. Consumer Product Safety Commission.

Bapuji, H., & Beamish, P. W. (2007, August 31). *Toy recalls—Is China the problem?* Retrieved September 11, 2007, from http://umanitoba.ca/news/images/toys_recalls_report.pdf

Barboza, D. (2006, October 13). Global companies fight Chinese effort on aiding unions. *International Herald Tribune.* Retrieved October 13, 2006, from http://www.iht.com

Barboza, D. (2007, September 11). Why lead in toy paint? It's cheaper. *The New York Times,* Retrieved September 11, 2007, from http://www.nytimes.com

Bhatia, S. J. (2007, September 12). *Testimony on enhancing the safety of our toys: Lead paint, the Consumer Product Safety Commission, and Toy Safety Standards.* Oral testimony of the American National Standards Institute before the U.S. Senate Appropriations Committee, Washington, DC.

Blanchette, J. (2007, July 2). Key issue for China's new labor law: Enforcement. *Christian Science Monitor.* Retrieved July 2, 2007, from http://www.csmonitor.com

Boston College Center for Corporate Citizenship. (2006). Corporate Citizen Management Framework. Retrieved September 15, 2006, from http://www.bcccc.net

Bradsher, K. (2007, November 30). Producer of poisonous toy beads issues apology. *The New York Times.* Retrieved November 30, 2007, from http://www.nytimes.com

Braidotti, R., Charkiewicz, E., Hausler, S., & Wieringa, S. (1994). *Women, the environment and sustainable development: Towards a theoretical synthesis.* London, UK: Zed Books.

158 / BEYOND CHILD'S PLAY

Bjurling, K. (2004). *Easy to manage—A report on Chinese toy workers and the responsibility of the companies.* Sweden: Swedwatch.

Cabot, H. (2005, December 14). Doll maker embarks on 'Save Girlhood' Campaign. ABC News. Retrieved June 15, 2006, from http://abcnews.go.com.

Cassady, A. (2005). *Trouble in toyland: 20th Annual Toy Safety Survey,* U.S. PIRG Education Fund, Washington, DC.

Chapman, J. (2005). *Emotionally durable design: Objects, experiences and empathy.* London, UK: Earthscan.

Childs, G. (1991). *Steiner education in theory and practice.* Trowbridge, UK: Floris Books.

China Labor Watch. (2005, September). *The toy industry in China: Undermining workers' rights and rule of law.* New York. Retrieved June 15, 2006, from http://www.chinalaborwatch.org.

Cohen, D. (2005). Globalization and employment. In P. Auer, G. Besse, & D. Méda (eds.), *Offshoring and the internationalization of employment–A challenge for a fair globalization?* Proceedings of the International Labour Organization Symposium, Annecy, France, 17-36.

Cross, G., & Smits, G. (2005). Japan, the US and the globalization of children's consumer culture. Pennsylvania State University. *Journal of Social History, 38*(4), 873-890.

Curtis, G. (Ed.). (1992). *East Germany: A country study.* Federal Research Division, Library of Congress, Washington, DC.

Datschefski, E. (1999, January). Cyclic, solar, safe-BioDesign's solution requirements for sustainability. *Journal of Sustainable Product Design, 8*, 42- 51.

Dee, J. (2007, December 23). A toy maker's conscience. *The New York Times Magazine.* Retrieved December 23, 2007, from http://www.nytimes.com

Delaney, H., & van de Zande, R. (Eds.). (2001). *A guide to the EU safety of toys.* National Institute of Standards and Technology, U.S. Department of Commerce, GCR 01-823.

Desai, M. (2002). Transnational solidarity: Women's agency, structural adjustment and globalization. In N. Naples & M. Desai (Eds.), *Women's activism and globalization: Linking local struggles and transnational politics* (pp. 15-33). New York: Routledge.

DiGangi, J., Schettler, T., Cobbing, M., & Rossi, R. (2002). *Aggregate exposures to phthalates in humans. Health care without harm.* Washington, DC. Retrieved January 15, 2008, from http://www.noharm.org

Dunn, K. (2006). What money can't buy. *Harvard Public Health Review,* Spring/Fall 2006 (pp. 17-18).

Edmondson, B. (2002, May/June). All dolled up. *Preservation Magazine.* Retrieved June 10, 2006, from http://www.geocities.com/saveheartsatwells/Rowland-Pres.html

Ekstrom, V. (2008, April 2). *States lead feds in toy safety.* Retrieved April 7, 2008, from http://www.stateline.org

Engardio, P. (2007, January 19). Beyond the green corporation: Moving away from platitudes to strategies that help world and bottom line. *Business Week.* Retrieved March 15, 2007, from http://www.msnbc.msn.com

Estremadoyro, J. (2001, June 21). Domestic violence in Andean communities of Peru. *Law, social justice and global development.* Retrieved April 7, 2006, from http://www2.warwick.ac.uk

Europe Economics. (2007, July 30). Revision of the chemical requirements of Directive 88/378/EEC on the safety of toys. Retrieved September 5, 2008, from http://ec.europa.eu/enterprise/toys/index_en.htm

Fiksel, J. (1996). *Design for environment: Creating eco-efficient products and processes.* New York: McGraw-Hill.

Foreman, W. (2008, October 19). Factory closure in China a sign of deeper pain. *The Associated Press.* Retrieved November 12, 2003, from http://ap.google/com

Formanek-Brunell, M. (1993). *Made to play house: Dolls and the commercialization of American girlhood, 1830-1930.* New Haven, CT: Yale University Press.

Fu, Y. (1998). Toyland inferno: A journey through the ruins—The story of Shenzhen's "Black Friday". *Chinese Sociology and Anthropology, 30*(4), 8-34.

Geiser, K. (2001). *Materials matter: Toward a sustainable materials policy.* Cambridge, MA: MIT Press.

Goddu, K. (2004). *Dollmakers and their stories: Women who changed the world of play.* New York: Henry Holt and Company.

Goldman, A. (2004, November 26). Sweat, fear and resignation amid all the toys: Despite Mattel's efforts to police factories, thousands of workers are suffering. *Los Angeles Times.* Retrieved June 10, 2006, from http://www.latimes.com

Goodfellow, C. (1993). *The ultimate doll book.* New York: Metro Books.

Goodman, P. (2006, January 30). In China, a rare return-lunar new year allows migrant workers to leave jobs in cities for rural homes. *The Washington Post.* Retrieved October 15, 2006, from http://www.washingtonpost.com

Graedel, T., & Allenby, B. (1996). *Design for environment.* Upper Saddle River, NJ: Prentice Hall.

Graham, L. (1995). *On the line at Subaru-Isuzu: The Japanese model and the American worker.* Ithaca, NY: Cornell University Press.

Grant, C. (1994). *Case study: The Kader toy factory fire.* International Labor Organization Report. Retrieved February 7, 2005, from http://www.ilo.org

Greiner, T., Rossi, M., Thorpe, B., & Kerr, B. (2006). *Healthy business strategies for transforming the toxic chemical economy.* Medford, MA: Clean Production Action. Retrieved September 8, 2006, from http://www.cleanproduction.org/healthybusiness.php

Handler, R. (1994). *Dream doll: The Ruth Handler story.* Stamford, CT: Longmeadow Press.

Hawken, P. (1993). *The ecology of commerce: A declaration of sustainability.* New York: HarperCollins.

Heckman, A. (2003). *Woven stories—Andean textiles and rituals.* Albuquerque: University of New Mexico Press.

Heer-Forsberg, M. (2005). American Girl, Inc. In M. Ferrara & J. Pederson (Eds.), *International directory of company histories* (Vol. 69, pp. 16-19). Detroit, MI: St. James Press. Retrieved June 2, 2006, from http://findarticles.com

Helmore, K., & Singh, N. (2001). *Sustainable livelihoods: Building on the wealth of the poor.* Bloomfield, CT: Kumarian Press.

Hillier, M. (1968). *Dolls and doll-makers.* New York: G. P. Putnam's Sons.

Holliday, C., & Pepper, J. (2002). *Sustainability through the market: Seven keys to success.* World Business Council on Sustainable Development. Retrieved September 15, 2006, from http://www.wbesd.ch

160 / BEYOND CHILD'S PLAY

Hong Kong Christian Industrial Committee [HKCIC]. (2001). How Hasbro, McDonald's, Mattel and Disney manufacture their toys. Hong Kong. Retrieved February 8, 2006, from http://www.cic.org.hk
International Labor Organization. (2006, April). *In the heart of the Sierra: Local talent at the service of the global economy.* Retrieved October 10, 2006, from http://www.ilo.org/public/english/bureau/inf/features/06/peru.htm
International Center for Corporate Accountability. (2008). Mattel's vendor plants—Compliance with Mattel's global manufacturing principles. Retrieved April 6, 2008, from http://www.icca-corporateaccountability.org/04_reports.php
ICCA. (2004, January 27). Mattel, Inc. Vendor plants in China—Audit report. Retrieved May 4, 2006, from http://www.icca-corporateaccountability.org/04_reports.php
ICCA. (2004, December 16). Follow-up audit of Mattel's China vendor operations, conducted July 28-August 2, 2004. Retrieved May 4, 2006, from http://www.icca-corporateaccountability.org/04_reports.php
ICCA. (2006a). Follow-up audit—Mattel's vendor plants 15, 16, 17. Retrieved May 14, 2006, from http://www.icca-corporateaccountability.org/04_reports.php
ICCA. (2006b). Mattel's vendor plants—Compliance with Mattel's global manufacturing principles. Retrieved May 14, 2006, from http://www.icca-corporateaccountability.org/04_reports.php
ICCA. (2006c, June 2). International Center for Corporate Accountability announces independent audit results for additional Mattel suppliers in China. Retrieved May 14, 2006, from http://www.icca-corporateaccountability.org/04_reports.php
International Council of Toy Industries [TCTI]. (2008). Frequently asked questions, Retrieved April 4, 2008, from http://www.icti-care.org/process/faq.html
Karasek, R. (1992). Stress prevention through work reorganization: A summary of 19 international case studies. *Conditions of Work Digest, 11*(2), 23-42.
Karasek, R. (1999). The new work organization and conducive value. *Dutch Sociological Journal, 5,* 310-330.
Kristof, N., & WuDunn, S. (2000). *Thunder from the East: Portrait of a rising Asia.* New York: Alfred A. Knopf.
Krombholz, M. (2001). *The story of German doll-making: 1530-2000.* Grantsville, MD: Hobby House Press.
Langer, B. (2004). The business of branded enchantment—Ambivalence and disjuncture in the global children's culture. *Journal of Consumer Culture, 4*(2), 251-277.
Law, C. K., & Chan, S. F. (2003). Panorama of toys design and development in Hong Kong. *Journal of Materials Processing Technology, 138,* 270-276.
Lewis, H., & Gertsakis, J. (2001). *Design + Environment: A global guide to designing greener goods.* Sheffield, UK: Greenleaf Publishing.
Lipton, E., & Story, L. (2007, September 7). Toy makers seek standards for US safety, *The New York Times.* Retrieved September 7, 2007, from http://www.cpsc.gov/cpscpub/prerel/category/toy.html
Living Planet Report. (2006). World Wildlife Fund, Zoological Society of London, and Global Footprint Network. Retrieved December 5, 2007, from http://www.panda.org
Lovaas, K. (1991, May). The dolls of Käthe Kruse—Yesterday and today (Part 2). *Dolls: The Collector's Magazine,* pp. 67-73.
MacPherson, M. (2004). *Sustainability for designers.* Report from the Natural Step—US. San Francisco, CA. Retrieved March 15, 2005, from www.naturalstep.org

Manno, J. (2002). Commoditization: Consumption efficiency and an economy of care and connection. In T. Princen, M. Maniates, & K. Conca (Eds.), *Confronting consumption* (pp. 67-99). Cambridge, MA: MIT Press.

Mattel. (2003a). *Corporate social responsibility report.* Retrieved June 4, 2006, from http://www.mattel.com

Mattel. (2003b). *Global Reporting Initiative (GRI) report.* Retrieved June 4, 2006, from http://www.mattel.com

McDonough, W., & Braungart, M. (2002). *Cradle to cradle: Remaking the way we make things.* New York: North Point Press.

McDonough, W., Braungart, M., Anastas, P., & Zimmerman, J. (2003, December 1). Applying the principles of green engineering to cradle-to-cradle design. *Environmental Science and Technology, 37*(23), 434-441.

McMichael, P. (2002). *Development and social change: A global perspective.* Thousand Oaks, CA: Pine Forge Press.

Messing, K. (1998). *One-eyed science: Occupational health and women workers.* Philadelphia, PA: Temple University Press.

Miller, G. W. (1998). *Toy wars: The epic struggle between G.I. Joe, Barbie and the companies that make them.* New York: Times Books.

Miller, J. (2001, June 1). Aurora in Rowland's Grip: Villagers fret over too much land, power in hands of one person. *The Citizen.* Retrieved July 15, 2006, from http://www.geocities.com

Morris, W. (Ed.). (1969). *The American Heritage Dictionary of the English Language.* Boston, MA: Houghton Mifflin Company.

Murray, L. (2002, September). Käthe Kruse, then and now. *Antique Doll Collector, 5*(8).

National Institute for Occupational Safety and Health. (2004, January). *A summary of health hazard evaluations: Issues related to occupational exposure to isocyanates, 1989 to 2002.* Cincinnati, OH: Department of Health and Human Services, Centers for Disease Control and Prevention.

National Labor Committee [NLC]. (2002). *Toys of misery: Made in China.* New York. Retrieved September 15, 2005, from http://www.nlcnet.org

National Labor Committee and China Labor Watch. (2004). *Toys of misery 2004.* New York. Retrieved September 15, 2005, from http://www.nlcnet.org

National Research Council. (1991). *Improving engineering design: Designing for competitive advantage.* Washington, DC: National Academy Press.

No storybook ending after tycoon dolls up village. (2007, October 14). Retrieved January 23, 2008, from http://www.cnn.com

NPD Group, Inc. (2008). *Toy markets in the world.* Prepared for ICTI by NPD. Retrieved December 9, 2008, from http://www.toyassociation.org

Pearson, J. (2006). *Design and sustainability: Opportunities for systemic transformation.* Retrieved April 1, 2006, from http://www.greenblue.org

Pereira, J. (2008, February 12). Protests spur stores to seek substitute for vinyl in toys. *The Wall Street Journal.* Retrieved February 18, 2008, from http://online.wsj.com

Petrash, J. 2002. *Understanding Waldorf education: Teaching from the inside out.* Beltsville, MD: Gryphon House, Inc.

Princen, T. (2002). Distancing: Consumption and the severing of feedback. In T. Princen, M. Maniates, & K. Conca (Eds.), *Confronting consumption* (pp. 103-131). Cambridge, MA: MIT Press.

Pyle, J. L., & Ward, K. B. (2003). Recasting our understanding of gender and work during global restructuring. *International Sociology, 18*(3), 461-489.

Quinn, M., Kriebel, D., Geiser, K., & Moure-Eraso, R. (1998). Sustainable production: A proposed strategy for the work environment. *American Journal of Industrial Medicine, 34,* 297-304.

Reinelt, S. (1994). *Käthe Kruse: The early years.* Duisburg: Verlag Puppen and Spielzeug.

Richter, L. (1984). *Treasury of Käthe Kruse dolls: Album 3.* Tucson, AZ: THP Books.

Roberts, D., & Engardio, P. (2006, November 27). Secrets, lies, and sweatshops. *Business Week.* Retrieved February 21, 2007, from http://www.msnbc.msn.com

Ross, J. (2001, November). *Poverty, empowerment and gendered life cycles: Latin American perspectives.* United Nations, Expert group meeting on empowerment of women throughout the life cycle as a transformative strategy for poverty eradication. Retrieved April 10, 2006, from http://www.un.org/womenwatch/daw/csw/empower/documents.html

Rossi, M., Tickner, J., & Geiser, K. (2006, July). *Alternatives assessment framework of the Lowell Center for Sustainable Production,* Version 1.0. Retrieved July 15, 2008, from www.chemicalspolicy.org

Rowland, P., & Sloane, J. (2002, October 1). A new twist on timeless toys. *Fortune Small Business.* Retrieved June 10, 2006, from http://money.cnn.com

Rowledge, L., Barton, R., & Brady, K. (1999). *Mapping the journey: Case studies in strategy and action toward sustainable development.* Sheffield, UK: Greenleaf Publishing.

Sanborn, M., Abelsohn, A., Campbell, M., & Weir, E. (2002). Identifying and managing adverse environmental health effects: 3. Lead exposure. *Canadian Medical Association Journal, 166*(10), 1287-1292.

Schor, J. (2005). *Born to buy: The commercialized child and the new consumer culture.* New York: Scribner.

Sethi, S. P. (2003). *Setting global standards—Guidelines for creating codes of conduct in multinational corporations.* Hoboken, NJ: John Wiley and Sons.

Steiner, R. (1996). *The education of the child and early lectures on education.* Hudson, NY: Anthroposophic Press.

Stern, S., & Schoenhaus, T. (1990). *Toyland: The high-stakes game of the toy industry.* Chicago, IL: Contemporary Books.

Story, L. (2007, August 20). After stumbling, Mattel cracks down in China. *The New York Times.* Retrieved August 29, 2007, from http://www.nytimes.com

Taylor, F. W. (1911). *The principles of scientific management.* Retrieved April 15, 2005, from http://www.fordham.edu/halsall/mod/1911taylor.html

Tickner, J. (1999). *A review of the availability of plastic substitutes for soft PVC in toys.* Greenpeace International. Retrieved May 10, 2006, from http://www.prcinformation.org/assets/pdf/PlasticSubstitutesPVCtoys_Tickner.pdf

Tickner, J., & Torrie, Y. (2008, February). *Presumption of safety: Limits of federal policies on toxic substances in consumer products.* Lowell Center for Sustainable Production, University of Massachusetts Lowell. Retrieved March 15, 2008, from http://www.sustainableproduction.org

Tischner, U., & Charter, M. (2001). Sustainable product design. In U. Tischner & M. Charter (Eds.), *Sustainable solutions: Developing products and services for the future* (pp. 118-138). Sheffield, UK: Greenleaf Publishing.

Tosa, M. (1997). *Barbie: Four decades of fashion, fantasy and fun.* New York: Harry Abrams, Inc.

Toy Industry Association, Inc. (2005). *A year in review: The growth, challenges and opportunities of the toy industry.* Retrieved July 10, 2006, from http://www.toy-tia.org/

Toy Safety Coordination Initiative. (2008, February 16). *Draft program recommendations.* Toy Industry Association and American National Standards Institute. Retrieved February 25, 2008, from http://www.ansi.org

Toys"R"Us. (2008, February 15). *Toys "R" Us announces further enhancements to its stringent product safety requirements.* Retrieved February 16, 2008, from www2.toysrus.com

United Nations Environmental Program [UNEP]. (2001). Consumption opportunities: Strategies for change—A report for decision-makers.

United Nations Environmental Program [UNEP]. (2002). Product—Service systems and sustainability: Opportunities for sustainable solutions. Retrieved April 5, 2005 from http://www.unep.fr/scp/design/pss.htm

U.S. Congress, Office of Technology Assessment. (1992). *Green products by design.* Washington, DC: U.S. Government.

U.S. Consumer Product Safety Commission Strategic Plan. (2003). Retrieved January 10, 2008 from http://www.cpsc.gov

U.S. Consumer Product Safety Commission. (1995). Retrieved June 10, 2006, from http://www.cpsc.gov

U.S. Department of State. (2008). Investment Climate Statement—Peru. Retrieved April 3, 2009 from www.state.gov

U.S. Environmental Protection Agency [US EPA]. (1994, December). *Aniline fact sheet—Support document.* OPPT Chemical Fact Sheets.

van Weenen, H. (1997). Sustainable product development: Opportunities for developing countries. In *Product development and the environment.* United Nations Environmental Program, Working Group on Sustainable Product Development, Division of Technology, Industry and Economics, *20,* no. 1-2.

Varadarajan, T. (2004, May 21). Shorn, shipped, censured—Why can't Jewish ladies wear Hindu hair? *The Wall Street Journal.* Retrieved January 15, 2006, from http://opinionjournal.com

Vernon, J., Nwaogu, T., Salado, R., Peacock, M., & Hayward, G. (2004). Study on the impact of the revision of the Council Directive 88/378/EEC on the safety of toys. Norfolk, UK: Risk and Policy Analysts Ltd.

Vinyl Toys are Safe. (2008). International Council of Toy Industries. Retrieved April 3, 2008, from http://www.toy-icti.org/resources/vinyl_toys.html

Voice of America News. *Many Peruvians struggle to gain health care access.* (2006, May 3). Retrieved May 3, 2006, from http://www.voanews.com/english/archive/2006-05/2006-05-03-voa41.cfm

Vogl, F. (2001). *Corporate integrity and globalization: The dawning of a new era of accountability and transparency.* Retrieved October 12, 2006, from http://www.ethics.org/resources/speech_detail.cfm?ID=33

Volvo. (2005). Cars Ghent: A self managing team model. In *EMCC company network—Workplace innovation: Four case examples.* European Foundation for the Improvement of Living and Working Conditions.

Walker, S., & Dorsa, E. (2001). Making design work: Sustainability, product design and social equity. *Journal of Sustainable Product Design, 1,* 41-48.

Walker, S. (2006). *Sustainable by design: Explorations in theory and practice.* London, UK: Earthscan.

Weidenhamer, J. D., & Clement, M. L. (2007, October). Leaded electronic waste is a possible source material for lead-contaminated jewelry. *Chemosphere, 69*(7), 1111-1115.

Wong, M., & Frost, S. (2000). *Monitoring Mattel: Codes of conduct, workers and toys in southern China.* Asia Monitor Resource Center, Hong Kong.

Young, R. (1992). *Dolls.* New York: Dillon Press.

Index

Chicago Botanic Garden, 52
China
    activism to improve working
        conditions, 23
    hazards in production, 14-15
    materials transported around the
        globe, 133
    polyvinyl chloride, 68
    produces most of U.S. toys, 12-13
    social impacts of globalization,
        129-130
    worker rights, 135
    working conditions in Chinese
        factories, 13-14, 23, 54-59
    See also American Girl doll company;
        Käthe Kruse doll company
China Labor Watch, 14, 54
China Toy Association, 12
Choking on small toy parts, 15
Christenson, Andrea, 62, 63,
    65-68, 82
Christenson, Steve, 62
Clean Production Action, 132
Codes of conduct/standards, 23-26
Cohen, Daniel, 133
Commerce Department, U.S., 20
Community development, sustainable, 4,
    41-42, 120, 153, 155, 156
    See also Q'ewar Project
Conceptual framework for sustainable
    product design
    eco-efficiency, 29-31
    key elements (5) of sustainable
        product design, 38-43
    life cycle of products, 31-33
    Natural Step framework for
        implementing sustainability, 38
    product-service systems, 32-33
    social/health aspects of production:
        environmental aspects of
        products, 36-38
    systems of sustainable
        production/consumption, 42
    terminology, history of: eco design
        concepts, 33-34
    Western model of economic growth is
        unsustainable, 29

Consumer culture, American, 16
Consumer Product Safety Commission
    (CPSC), 15, 16, 18-19, 145
Consumers Union, 20
Converse, 142
Cradle to Cradle Design, 35
Craft production, 126
    See also American Girl doll company;
        Käthe Kruse doll; Q'ewar Project

Datschefski, Edwin, 35
Demand/control model to predict
    job-related stress, 37
Design + Environment (Lewis &
    Gertsakis), 37
*Design for Environment: Creating
    Eco-Efficient Products and
    Processes* (Fiksel), 34
Design for environment (DFE), 34-35,
    141
    See also American Girl doll company;
        Käthe Kruse doll; Q'ewar Project
Design for Environment (Graedel &
    Allenby), 34-35
Dignity, designing work for human, 124,
    127-130
Di-isononyl phthalate (DINP), 16-17
Direct mail advertising, 48
Diversity and eco-effective design, 35
Domestic violence, 87
Dorsa, Ed, 37

Eco design, 34-36
Eco-efficiency, 29-31, 35
Eco-labeled fabrics, 22
Economically viable, products as
    design, framework for sustainable
        product, 41, 42
    emerging themes for sustainable
        product design, 136-137
    Q'ewar Project, 114-116, 124
    social/health aspects of production:
        environmental aspects of
        products, 153-156

Mattel, 3, 6, 13, 15-16, 26-27, 45,
131-133
See also American Girl doll company
McDonough, William, 30, 35
Meaning in doll design, imbedded, 5-6
Methylene diphenyl diisocyanate (MDI),
82
MGA Entertainment, 50

National Bureau of Standards, 20
National Labor Committee (NLC), 13, 14,
25, 54
National Research Council (NRC), 33
National Safety Council, 20
Natural Step framework for implementing
sustainability, 38
Nature Net, 50
New York Times, 117
Nickels, Christa, 23
Nike, 12
Nova Natural, 114

Office of Technology Assessment (OTA),
U.S. Congress, 33-34
Öko-Tex Standard 100, 22, 66, 123

Pacific Crest Outward Bound, 52
Paradigm shifting/incremental change:
sustainability/design/production/
consumption
connecting the term sustainable to
product, 139-140
design for environment, 141
emotionally durable design, 144
functionality/aesthetics/quality, 139
integrated product development,
144-148
labeling, independent third-party, 146
life-cycle of products, designing for
the, 143
linking sustainable product
design/production/consumption,
143-149
sustainability/design/production/
consumption]
purpose of a product, what is the,
140-141

[Paradigm shifting/incremental change:
sustainability/design/production/
consumption]
safety/health issues, 145-146
scale, the challenges of, 141-143
social responsibility, 148
summary/conclusions, 148-149
transparency about
environmental/social costs of
products, 147
Peru. *See* Q'ewar Project
Philippines, 133
Phthalates, 16-17, 20, 24
Plastics used more after World War II, 9
Pleasant Company, 3
Pleasant T. Rowland Foundation, 51
Polyol, 82
Polystyrene, 82, 132
Polyvinyl chloride (PVC), 2-3, 15, 16, 24,
68, 122, 132
Privatization of public functions, 12
Product-service systems, 32-33
Public Interest Research Group, U.S.
(PIRG), 24
Pyle, Jean, 11

Q'ewar Project
community development, sustainable,
4, 113
design process, 89-90
dignity, human, 124
economics of the, 114-116, 124
fiber inhalation, 96
founders (Julio Herrera and Lucy
Terrazas), 86, 97
initiation of the, 87-89
job rotation/variation, 94
materials used, 94-95
new directions for, 116
overview, 85-87
plant-based dyes, 93
production process, 90-96, 100-109
repetitive motion injuries, 96
safety/health issues, 96, 113
special aspects of the, 96, 113
staff picture, 98